Spoken English
A Manual of Speech and Phonetics

Fifth Edition

R. K. Bansal, Ph. D. (London)
formerly, Professor of Phonetics and Spoken English
The English and Foreign Languages University
Hyderabad, India

J. B. Harrison, M. A. (Oxon)
formerly, Lecturer, School of Education
University of Leicester, U. K.
and
Visiting Professor of Spoken English
The English and Foreign Languages University
Hyderabad, India

Orient BlackSwan

All rights reserved. No part of this book may be modified, reproduced or utilised in any form, or by any means, electronic or mechanical, including photocopying, recording or by any information storage and retrieval system, in any form of binding or cover other than in which it is published, without permission in writing from the publisher.

SPOKEN ENGLISH (FIFTH EDITION)

ORIENT BLACKSWAN PRIVATE LIMITED

Registered Office
3-6-752, Himayatnagar, Hyderabad 500 029, Telangana, India
e-mail: centraloffice@orientblackswan.com

Other Offices
Bengaluru, Chennai, Guwahati, Hyderabad, Kolkata,
Mumbai, New Delhi, Noida, Patna

© Orient Blackswan Private Limited 1972, 1983, 1994, 2013, 2024
First Published 1972
Reprinted 1974, 1976
Second Edition 1983
Reprinted 1986, 1991, 1992, 1993
Third Edition 1994
Reprinted 1995, 1996, 1997, 1998, 1999, 2000, 2001, 2002, 2003, 2004, 2005, 2006, 2008, 2009, 2010
Fourth Edition 2013
Reprinted 2014, 2015, 2016, 2018, 2019, 2022
Fifth Edition 2024

Cover and book design
© Orient Blackswan Private Limited 2024

ISBN: 978-93-5442-980-4

Typeset in IPAphon 11/14.2 *by*
Orient BlackSwan

Printed in India at
Shree Maitrey Printech Pvt. Ltd., Noida 201301

Published by
Orient Blackswan Private Limited
3-6-752, Himayatnagar, Hyderabad 500 029 Telangana, India
e-mail: info@orientblackswan.com

Contents

Publisher's Note   vii
Preface   ix
List of Phonetic Symbols and Signs   xi

Part I   Phonetics and Spoken English

1. **Introduction**   1
   1.1   Language   1
   1.2   The English Language   1
   1.3   Spoken English in India   1
   1.4   Learning a Foreign Language   2

2. **The Speech Mechanism**   5
   2.1   A Speech Event   5
   2.2   The Production of Speech   5
   2.3   Description of Sounds   7

3. **The Description of Speech Sounds**   8
   3.1   Vowels and Consonants   8
   3.2   Description of Consonants   8
   3.3   Description of Vowels   11
   3.4   Use of Phonetic Symbols   12

4. **The Phoneme, the Syllable and Prosodic Features**   13
   4.1   The Phoneme   13
   4.2   The Syllable   14
   4.3   Prosodic Features   14

5. **The Sounds of English: Vowels**   15
   5.1   Vowels in British Received Pronunciation   15
   5.2   Vowels in General Indian English   16
   5.3   Differences between the Vowel Systems of British R. P. and General Indian English   17

5.4 Description of the Vowels 18

6. **The Sounds of English— Consonants** 61
   6.1 Introduction 61
   6.2 Plosives 61
   6.3 Affricates 68
   6.4 Fricatives 69
   6.5 Nasals 77
   6.6 Lateral /l/ 79
   6.7 Post-alveolar Frictionless Continuant /r/ 81
   6.8 Semi-Vowels 81
   6.9 Consonant Clusters 83

7. **Word Stress** 89
   7.1 Word Stress 89
   7.2 Stress Shift 90
   7.3 Historical Reasons for Shift 91
   7.4 Compound Words 91
   7.5 Stress Change According to Function 92
   7.6 Word Stress in Indian English 93
   7.7 Rules for Stress Patterns 93

8. **Features of Connected Speech** 96
   8.1 Stress in Connected Speech : Rhythm 96
   8.2 Weak Forms 101
   8.3 Intonation 105

9. **Factors Affecting the International Intelligibility of Indian English and Suggestions for Improvement** 116
   9.1 Features that Affect the Intelligibility of Indian English 116

Part II Exercises for Practice

10. Vowels   125
11. Consonants   149
12. Consonant Clusters   175
13. Conversations   193

A Select Bibliography   220

Publisher's Note

This book has been written for the use of teachers and students in India who wish to improve their pronunciation in English and acquire the correct patterns of accent, rhythm and intonation.

The standard of pronunciation aimed at is based on accepted Indian usage modified in the direction of British Received Pronunciation to attain international intelligibility.

The description of British R. P. and the symbols used for R. P. phonemes are based on those given in Professor A. C. Gimson's *An Introduction to the Pronunciation of English* (Edward Arnold). In so many other places throughout the book, Professor Gimson's influence will be obvious.

The statements about Indian English and about features that are likely to make it unintelligible to native English speakers are based on Professor R. K. Bansal's research on the intelligibility of Indian English conducted at the University of London during the period 1964–66 under Professor Gimson's guidance.

Part I contains a brief introduction to phonetics and information about the sound system of English. Part II contains useful exercise material for pronunciation drills and conversation practice.

Mr C. Brasnett, formerly Visting Reader in Phonetics and Spoken English at the English and Foreign Languages University, Hyderabad, very kindly checked the stress and tone marks in the exercise material in the first edition of the book. The publishers are deeply grateful to Dr Kamlesh Sadanand, former Professor and Head, Department of Phonetics and Spoken English, the English and Foreign Languages University,

Hyderabad, for working on the revision of the third edition in consultation with Dr Brian Harrison.

The revised editions incorporate a number of amendments based on the authors' experience on courses in phonetics and spoken English.

In the fifth edition of the book, the audio components may be accessed through the app accompanying the book. The instructions for using the app are given on the inside front cover of the book.

Preface

Spoken English was first published in 1972 as *Spoken English for India*, and now, more than forty years later, we are embarking on the fourth edition of the book. Between then and now there have been twenty reprints. The book can, therefore, be said to have stood the test of time and to have influenced several generations of students of English. There have been many changes in India and in Indian society since 1972, even though much perhaps has remained the same. Amongst the changes has been the rise of a large anglophone middle class, at best speaking English at a level of international intelligibility, at worst relying on a dialect incomprehensible to all except the speaker's home group. Not that I have anything against dialects—I speak one myself when I go back to my native village in the English Lake District. Historically, my accent descends in direct line from that spoken by the romantic poet Wordsworth. I have become bidialectal, speaking something much closer to Received Pronunciation when not in my village. A former principal of mine Professor V. K. Gokak of what was then the Central Institute of English in Hyderabad used to speak of English as India's 'window on the world.' This reflected the thinking of the time, but English in India is now much more powerful. India is now inside the English speaking world looking out, not an aspirant to that world looking in.

As India has changed, so has this book. In particular, the practice material has been revised. Some dialogues have been removed completely, others modified, to reflect the changing conditions in which English operates. All the spoken material—drills and dialogues—has been placed on a CD to provide models of English spoken at a level of international intelligibility.

I would like to thank Dr Kamlesh Sadanand for her invaluable help in the preparation of the revised edition. Any problems that arose did because we were operating at a distance of fifteen thousand miles from each other, in different hemispheres and across several time zones. Finally, I would like to salute the memory of the late Dr R. K. Bansal. This book is part of his legacy.

Patagonia, Argentina   **Brian Harrison**
January 2013

List of Phonetic Symbols and Signs

Vowels (British Received Pronunciation)

Pure Vowels: 12

/iː/	as in	these	/ðiːz/
/ɪ/	as in	bit	/bɪt/
/e/	as in	bed	/bed/
/æ/	as in	bad	/bæd/
/ʌ/	as in	bus	/bʌs/
/ɑː/	as in	card	/kɑːd/
/ɒ/	as in	hot	/hɒt/
/ɔː/	as in	all	/ɔːl/
		force	/fɔːs/
		horse	/hɔːs/
/ʊ/	as in	book	/bʊk/
/uː/	as in	rule	/ruːl/
		tube	/tjuːb/
/ɜː/	as in	serve	/sɜːv/
/ə/	as in	account	/əˈkaʊnt/
		drama	/ˈdrɑːmə/

Vowel Glides: 8

/eɪ/	as in	gate	/geɪt/
/aɪ/	as in	bite	/baɪt/
/ɔɪ/	as in	boil	/bɔɪl/
/əʊ/	as in	home	/həʊm/
/aʊ/	as in	house	/haʊs/
/ɪə/	as in	cheer	/tʃɪə/
/ɛə/	as in	air	/ɛə/
/ʊə/	as in	poor	/pʊə/

Vowels (General Indian English accepted usage)

Pure Vowels: 11

/iː/	as in	these	/d̪iːz/
/ɪ/	as in	bit	/bɪt/
/eː/	as in	gate	/geːt/
/ɛ/	as in	bed	/bɛd/
/æː/	as in	bad	/bæd/
/aː/	as in	card	/kaːrd/
		drama	[ˈdraːma]
/ɒ/	as in	hot	/hɒt/
		all	/ɒl/, [ɒːl]
		horse	/hɒrs/
/oː/	as in	home	/hoːm/
		force	/foːrs/
/ʊ/	as in	book	/bʊk/
/uː/	as in	rule	/ruːl/
		tube	/tjuːb/
/ə/	as in	bus	/bəs/
		serve	/sərv/
		account	/əˈkaʊnt/

Vowel Glides: 6

/aɪ/	as in	bite	/baɪt/
/ɔɪ/	as in	boil	/bɔɪl/
/aʊ/	as in	house	/haʊs/
/ɪə/	as in	cheer	/tʃɪər/
/eə/	as in	air	/eər/
/ʊə/	as in	poor	/pʊər/

Consonants

				British R. P.	Indian English
/p/	as in		pen	/pen/	/pɛn/
/b/	as in		bag	/bæg/	/bæg/
/t̪ʰ/	as in	Indian	thank	—	/t̪ʰæŋk/
/d̪/	as in	Indian	then	—	/d̪ɛn/
/t/	as in		take	/teɪk/	teːk/
/d/	as in		day	/deɪ/	/deː/
/k/	as in		keep	/kiːp/	/kiːp/
/g/	as in		gate	/geɪt/	geːt/
/tʃ/	as in		chain	/tʃeɪn/	/tʃeːn/
/dʒ/	as in		join	/dʒɔɪn/	/dʒɔɪn/
/f/	as in		face	/feɪs/	/feːs/
/v/	as in	British R. P.	vain	/veɪn/	—
/θ/	as in	British R. P.	thank	/θæŋk/	—
/ð/	as in	British R. P.	then	/ðen/	—
/s/	as in		sea	/siː/	/siː/
/z/	as in		zoo	/zuː/	/zuː/
/ʃ/	as in		shade	/ʃeɪd/	/ʃeːd/
/ʒ/	as in		measure	/ˈmeʒə/	/ˈmɛʒər/
/h/	as in		hand	/hænd/	/hænd/
/m/	as in		make	/meɪk/	/meːk/
/n/	as in		night	/naɪt/	/naɪt/
/ŋ/	as in		long	/lɒŋ/	/lɒŋ/
/l/	as in		lamp	/læmp/	/læmp/
/ʋ/	as in	Indian	vain	—	/ʋeːn/
		Indian	wait	—	/ʋeːt/
/r/	as in		rain	/reɪn/	reːn/
/j/	as in		yes	/jes/	/jɛs/
/w/	as in	British R. P.	wait	/weɪt/	

Other Symbols

p^h	voiceless aspirated bilabial plosive: e.g. Hindi फ
b^h	voiced aspirated bilabial plosive: e.g. Hind भ
t̪	voiceless dental plosive: e.g. Hindi त
t^h	voiceless aspirated alveolar plosive
ṭ	voiceless retroflex plosive: e.g. Hindi ट frequently used in India for English /t/
ḍ	voiced retroflex plosive: e.g. Hindi ड frequently used in India for English /d/
k^h	voiceless aspirated velar plosive: e.g. Hindi रव
ɫ	velarised /l/
$ʊ^h$	aspirated /ʊ/

Signs

/ /	phonemic transcription
[ ]	phonetic transcription
~	nasalization
h	aspiration
◌̪	dental articulation
ː	indicates length of preceding vowel
ˈ	main accentual stress or pitch prominence on following syllable
ˌ	secondary accentual stress on following syllable
\	high falling pitch
\	low falling pitch
/	high rising pitch
/	low rising pitch
∨	falling rising pitch

Part I
Phonetics and Spoken English

1. Introduction

1.1 Language

Language is a system of communication through speech, and written language is an attempt to represent the spoken language by visual symbols. In English, the correspondence between the written form and the spoken form is not consistently maintained. It is therefore necessary for Indian students to make a systematic study of the English sound system—the *phonetics* of English—and avoid any prejudices arising out of their study of written English.

1.2 The English Language

English has spread to and is spoken over such a large part of the world that native speakers have developed slightly different accents in the USA, UK, Canada, Australia and New Zealand; and a large number of non-native accents have come into existence as well, each influenced by features of the speaker's first language.

1.3 Spoken English in India

English as spoken by educated people in India does not differ radically from native English in grammar and vocabulary, but in pronunciation it is different from both British and American English. Even within India there are a large number of regional varieties, each different from the other in certain ways, and retaining to some extent the phonetic patterns of the Indian language spoken in that particular region. These regional varieties of English are sometimes not even mutually intelligible.[1] In every region, however, there are people who have shaken off the gross features of regional accent and speak a more 'neutral' form of Indian English. It is also true that in every region there are good speakers of English and bad speakers of English, the terms 'good' and 'bad' referring to the degrees of approximation to native English and Standard Indian English and also to qualities of clear, effective and intelligible speech. It would, however, be better to aim at international intelligibility.

1.4 Learning a Foreign Language

Language learning involves the reproduction by learners of the sounds and patterns used by other human beings around them. In learning to speak the second language, however, learners are influenced by the system of their own language and tend to hear and speak the foreign language in terms of the system of the former. In order to minimise this influence, therefore, it is necessary for us as foreign language learners to recognise the difference between the system of our first language and that of the foreign language we learn.

---

[1] Bansal, R.K., *The Intelligibility of Indian English*, University of London, Ph.D. thesis, 1966, Vol. 1, pp. 38–39.

2. The Speech Mechanism

2.1 A Speech Event

A speech event happens as a result of a number of processes. A concept is first formulated in the speaker's brain and its linguistic codification transmitted by the nerves to the speech organs, which are set in motion. The movements of these organs set up disturbances in the air, and these sound waves are received by the listener's ear. His nervous system carries the message to the brain, where it is interpreted in linguistic terms. The speaker and the listener must share the same linguistic code in order to communicate effectively.

2.2 The Production of Speech

The energy for the production of speech is generally provided by the air-stream coming out of the lungs.

At the top of the wind-pipe or the *trachea*, is the *larynx* or 'voice box' containing the *vocal cords*. These can be brought together or kept apart, the opening between them being called the *glottis*.

When we cough, the glottis is tightly closed and the air from the lungs is held up beneath it and then suddenly released. When we breathe out, the glottis is held open. If the vocal cords are held sufficiently close together, they vibrate when the air from the lungs passes between them. This vibration produces *voice*. Speech sounds can be *voiced* or *voiceless*.

The air-stream is also modified by the resonating cavities above the larynx—the pharynx, the mouth and the nasal cavity.

The shape of the mouth cavity depends on the positions of the *tongue* and the *lips*. The roof of the mouth is divided into three parts: the *alveolar ridge* or *teeth ridge* just behind the upper teeth; the *hard palate*; and the *soft palate* or *velum*, the end of which is called the *uvula*.

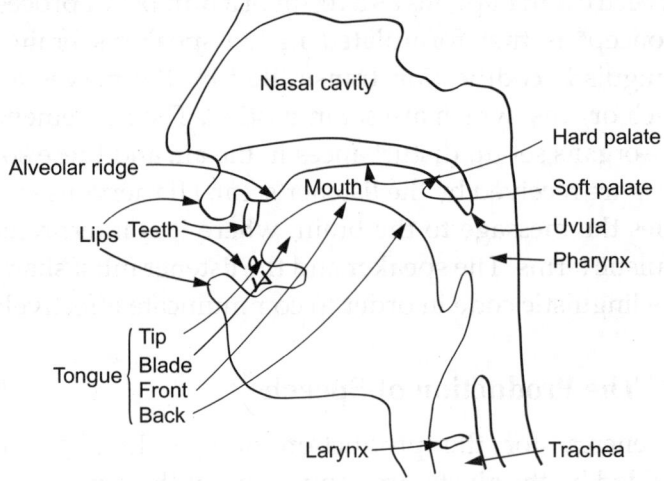

Fig. 1 Organs of Speech

The soft palate can be lowered to let the air escape through the nose. This is the normal position in breathing. If the mouth passage is also open, a *nasalised* vowel, as in Hindi /hæ̃/ 'are' is produced. If no air escapes through the mouth, a *nasal consonant* is produced, e.g., English /m/ and /n/ in *man* /mæn/, and /ŋ/ in *sing* /sɪŋ/.

The lips can be held close together or far apart. They can be *spread, neutral, open* or *rounded*.

The tongue can be considered as having three sections. The part opposite the teeth-ridge is called the *blade*, its end being called the *tip*. The part opposite the hard palate is called the *front* and that opposite the soft palate is called the *back*.

In the production of vowel sounds, the tip of the tongue is generally kept low, and some other part of the tongue—the front, the centre or the back—is raised towards the roof of the mouth.

The various parts of the tongue can make a contact with, or be brought very near the roof of the mouth to produce different consonant sounds.

2.3 Description of Sounds

In order to describe the production of a speech sound we have to indicate the nature of the air stream, the state of the vocal cords, and the .positions of the soft palate, the tongue and the lips.

3. The Description of Speech Sounds

3.1 Vowels and Consonants

It is usual to divide all speech sounds into two broad categories—vowels and consonants. In the production of vowels, the air comes out freely through the mouth. There is no closure of the air-passage and no narrowing of the passage that would cause audible friction. All other sounds are called consonants.

3.2 Description of Consonants

While describing consonants we have to indicate
- the nature of the air-stream:
  - whether it is *pulmonic* (set in motion by the lungs) or not.
  - whether it is *egressive* (coming out) or *ingressive*.
- whether the sound is *voiced* or *voiceless*, that is, whether the vocal cords vibrate or not.
- whether the soft palate is raised or lowered, that is, whether the air-stream passes
  - through the mouth only (*oral* sounds);
  - through the nose only (*nasal* sounds); or
  - through both the mouth and the nose (*nasalised* sounds).

- the place of articulation, that is, where the closure or narrowing takes place.
- the manner of articulation, that is, the kind of closure or narrowing.

All English sounds are produced with egressive lung air. Some English consonants are voiceless; these are /p, t, k, tʃ, f, θ, s, ʃ, h/. Others are voiced, namely, /b, d, g, dʒ, v, ð, z, ʒ, m, n, ŋ, l, r, j, w/.

3.2.1 Place of Articulation

Consonants can be classified according to the place of articulation as follows:

bilabial	– articulated by the two lips, e.g., English /p, b, m, w/.
labio-dental	– articulated by the lower lip against the upper teeth, e.g., English /f, v/, Hindi and Indian English /ʋ/.
dental	– articulated by the tip of the tongue against the upper teeth, e.g., English /θ, ð/, Hindi and Indian English /t̪ʰ, d̪/.
alveolar	– articulated by the blade of the tongue against the teeth-ridge, e.g., English /t, d, s, z, n, l/.
post-alveolar	– articulated by the tip of the tongue against the back of the teeth-ridge, e.g., English /r/.
retroflex	– articulated by the tip of the tongue curled back against the front of the hard palate, e.g. Hindi /ʈ, ɖ/.
palato-alveolar	– articulated by the blade of the tongue against the teeth-ridge, with the front of the tongue raised towards the hard palate, e.g., English /tʃ, dʒ, ʃ, ʒ/.

palatal — articulated by the front of the tongue against the hard palate, e.g., English /j/.

velar — articulated by the back of the tongue against the soft plate, e.g., English /k, g, ŋ/.

glottal — produced by an obstruction or narrowing between the vocal cords, e.g., English /h/.

3.2.2 Manner of Articulation

The closure at the place of articulation can be either complete or partial, or there may be only a narrowing that causes friction.

Consonants can be classified according to the manner of articulation as follows:

plosive: There is a complete closure of the air-passage; pressure is built up, and then the air is released with explosion, e.g., English /p, b, t, d, k, g/, Hindi and Indian English /ṭʰ, ḍ/.

affricate: There is a complete closure of the air passage in the mouth; then the organs are separated slowly so that friction is heard, e.g., English /tʃ, dʒ/.

nasal: There is a complete closure of the air passage in the mouth; the soft palate is lowered and the air escapes through the nose, e.g., English /m, n, ŋ/.

roll: There are a number of rapid taps made by a flexible organ against a firmer surface. For example, some people pronounce English /r/ by making the tip of the tongue strike against the teeth-ridge a number of times.

flap: There is only one tap; for example English /r/ in *very* is pronounced by making one tap of the tip of the tongue against the teeth-ridge.

lateral: At some point in the mouth, there is a closure in the middle, but the air escapes through the sides, e.g., English /l/.

fricative: There is a narrow passage for the air between two organs, and friction is produced when the air passes through it, e.g., English /f, v, θ ð, s, z. ʃ, ʒ, h/, English /r/ in words like *train* and *draw*.

frictionless continuant: There is no closure or friction, but the sound has a consonantal function, e.g., English /r/ in words like *rain, red*, etc., and Hindi and Indian English /ʋ/.

semi-vowel: A vowel glide with a consonantal function, e.g., English /j, w/.

3.3 Description of Vowels

In the production of vowels the air from the lungs comes out in a continuous stream through the mouth, and the vocal cords vibrate to produce 'voice'. There is no closure of the air passage and no narrowing that would cause friction. The note produced by the larynx is modified by the shapes of the resonating cavities of the pharynx, the mouth and the nose. These in turn depend on the positions of the soft palate, the tongue and the lips.

The soft palate is raised for oral vowels; all English vowels are oral. If the soft palate is lowered, we get nasalised vowels, which are used in Hindi, for instance.

Except for the tip and blade of the tongue which are not used for the production of vowels, any other part of the tongue can be raised towards the roof of the mouth, and there can be different degrees of raising of the tongue. Vowels in the production of which the highest part of the tongue is the front are called *front* vowels, e.g., English (R.P.[1]) /iː, ɪ, e, æ, ʌ/; those in which it is the back are called *back* vowels, e.g., English (R.P.) /ɑː, ɒ, ɔː, ʊ, uː/; and those in which it is the centre are called *central* vowels, e.g. English (R.P.)

---
[1]See Section 5.1

/ɜː, ə/. According to the degree of raising of the tongue, vowels are divided into four categories—*close* (as near as possible to the roof of the mouth without causing friction or making a closure), e.g., English /iː, uː/; *half-close*; *half-open*; and *open* (as low as possible, e.g., English (R.P.) /ɑː, ɒ/)

The lips can be *spread*, as for English /iː/; *neutral*, as for English (R.P.) /e/; *open*, as for English (R.P.) /ɑː/; *open rounded*, as for English (R.P.) /ɒ/; or *close rounded*, as for English /uː/.

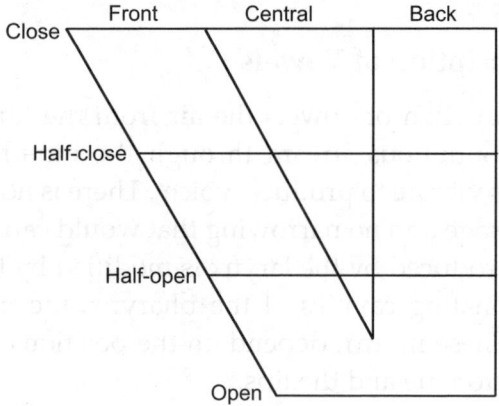

Fig. 2 Classification of Tongue Positions for Vowels

If the quality of a vowel does not change, it is sometimes called a *pure* vowel, e.g., English (R.P.) /iː, ɑː, ɔ., uː/. Vowels which involve a gliding movement from one quality to another are called *diphthongs*, if the glide takes place within the same syllable.

3.4 Use of Phonetic Symbols

It is convenient to use the phonetic symbols suggested by the International Phonetic Association to represent the sounds of speech.

4. The Phoneme, the Syllable and Prosodic Features

4.1 The Phoneme

Every language. has a limited number of distinctive sound-units called *phonemes*. They are distinctive in that they are the smallest units in the sound system of a language which can be used to differentiate meanings. *Minimal pairs* in a language i.e. pairs of words which differ only in one sound segment can often help us to identify the phonemes of that language.

A series like *pet, bet, debt, get, jet, vet, set, met, net, let, yet, wet,* gives us a list of twelve English phonemes /p, b, d, g, dʒ, v, s, m, n, l, j, w/. Other phonemes can be found by similar substitutions in various positions.

Each phoneme may have a number of variants called *allophones* which may occur as a result of the influence of adjacent vowels or consonants in a word or their position in a word i.e. initial or final. For example, the voiced post-alveolar frictionless continuant /r/ in British English is realised as a voiced fricative when used after /d/ and a voiceless fricative when used after stressed /p, t, k/. Thus in the words *dream, draw* and *dry*, the voiced fricative [r] is an allophone of the post-alveolar frictionless continuant / r /which is a phoneme in English. Similarly in the words *pack, tail, case,* the aspirated /p^h, t^h, k^h/ are allophones of the phonemes /p, t, k/.

4.2 The Syllable

One or more phonemes form the next higher unit called the *syllable*. In each syllable there is one sound that is more prominent than the rest. Usually it is a vowel, e.g., /iː/ in *beat* /biːt/, but in English it can also be a consonant, e.g., / n / and / l / in the second syllable of *cotton* (R. P. /kɒtn/ and *table* (R. P. /ˈteɪbl/), if we do not pronounce the potential vowel sound / ə / between / t / and / n / in /ˈkɒtn / and / b / and / l / in /ˈteɪbl /. In the English Pronouncing Dictionary (17th edition) the vowel / ə / is given as optional in /ˈkɒtᵊn/ and /ˈteɪbᵊl/ which means that if we were to pronounce the vowel /ə/ in both the words / n / and / l / would no longer occupy the central position in the second syllable.

The syllables in a language have their own patterns of structure. Vowels generally take the central position in the syllable, and consonants take the marginal positions. In other words, it would be difficult to produce a syllable or a single-syllable word without a vowel sound. The vowel in an English word is therefore, obligatory.

4.3 Prosodic Features

Features which relate to an utterance longer than a sound segment are called *supra-segmental* or *prosodic*. These include *length, stress* and *pitch*. The term 'length' relates to duration which indicates the time taken to utter a sound up to the beginning of the following sound in a word. Stress relates to the greater breath force used by a speaker on a particular syllable and in a word as compared to the other syllables in that word. It involves the use of greater muscular energy which generally results in an increase in air pressure. Pitch relates to the note of the voice as determined by the frequency of vibration of the vocal cords, i.e. the higher the frequency of the vibration, the higher the pitch, and the lower the frequency, the lower the pitch.

5. The Sounds of English: Vowels

5.1 Vowels in British Received Pronunciation

There are twenty distinct vowels in British Received Pronunciation (R.P.). Received Pronunciation, or Educated Southern British English, is a form of English socially acceptable (well received) in all parts of the country. The twenty vowels are:

Pure Vowels

/iː/	as in	these	/ðiːz/
/ɪ/	as in	bit	/bɪt/
/e/	as in	bed	/bed/
/æ/	as in	bad	/bæd/
/ʌ/	as in	bus	/bʌs/
/ɑː/	as in	card	/kɑːd/
/ɒ/	as in	hot	/hɒt/
/ɔː/	as in	all	/ɔːl/
		force	/fɔːs/
		horse	/hɔːs/
/ʊ/	as in	book	/bʊk/
/uː/	as in	rule	/ruːl/
		tube	/tjuːb/
/ɜː/	as in	serve	/sɜːv/
/ə/	as in	account	/əˈkaʊnt/

Vowel Glides			
/eɪ/	as in	gate	/geɪt/
/aɪ/	as in	bite	/baɪt/
/ɔɪ/	as in	boil	/bɔɪl/
/əʊ/	as in	home	/həʊm/
/aʊ/	as in	house	/haʊs/
/ɪə/	as in	cheer	/tʃɪə/
/ɛə/	as in	air	/ɛə/
/ʊə/	as in	poor	/pʊə/

Seven of these vowels — /ɪ, e, æ, ʌ, ɒ, ʊ, ə/ — are short, and the others are long. Among the long vowels, five — /iː, ɑː, ɔː, uː, ɜː/ — are monophthongs (sometimes called pure vowels), and the others are diphthongs (vowel glides within the syllable). Three of the diphthongs — /eɪ, aɪ, ɔɪ/ — involve glides to /ɪ/, two — /əʊ, aʊ/ — involve glides to /ʊ/ and the remaining three — /ɪə, ɛə, ʊə/ — are glides to /ə/.

5.2 Vowels in General Indian English

Corresponding to the twenty-vowel system of British R.P., General Indian English generally has a system of 11 pure vowels and 6 vowel glides. These are:

Pure Vowels			
/iː/[1]	as in	these	/d̪iːz/
/ɪ/	as in	bit	/bɪt/
/eː/	as in	gate	/geːt/
/ɛ/	as in	bed	/bɛd/
/æ/	as in	bad	/bæd/
/aː/	as in	card	/kaːrd/
/ɒ/	as in	hot	/hɒt/
		all	[ɒːl]
		horse	/hɒrs/

[1] Long vowels tend to have reduced length in unaccented syllables

/ɔː/	as in	home	/hoːm/
		force	/fɔːrs/
/ʊ/	as in	book	/bʊk/
/uː/	as in	rule	/ruːl/
		tube	/tjuːb/
/ə/	as in	bus	/bəs/
		bird	/bərd/
		account	/əˈkaʊnt/

Vowel Glides

/aɪ/	as in	bite	/baɪt/
/ɔɪ/	as in	boil	/bɔɪl/
/aʊ/	as in	house	/haʊs/
/ɪə/	as in	cheer	/tʃɪər/
/eə/	as in	air	/eər/
/ʊə/	as in	poor	/pʊər/

5.3 Differences between the Vowel Systems of British R.P. and General Indian English

The important differences between the vowel systems of British R.P. and General Indian English are as follows:

- Indian English has only one phoneme /ə/ corresponding to R.P. /ʌ/, /ɜː/ and /ə/.
- Indian English has one phoneme /ɒ/ corresponding to R.P. /ɒ/ and /ɔː/.
- Indian English has monophthongs /eː/ and /oː/ in place of R.P. diphthongs /eɪ/ and /əʊ/.
- The qualities of some of the Indian English vowels are different from those in R.P.
- The distribution of vowels in Indian English sometimes differs from that in R.P. For example, in R.P. generally a

weak vowel — /ə/, /ɪ/ or /ʊ/ — is used in an unstressed syllable. This is not the case in Indian English, where the tendency is to use the vowel indicated by the spelling.

5.4 Description of the Vowels

Brief articulatory descriptions of English vowels are given here, along with information about spellings and common substitutions in Indian English. Exercises for practising these vowels and the important phonemic contrasts are given in Part II of the book.

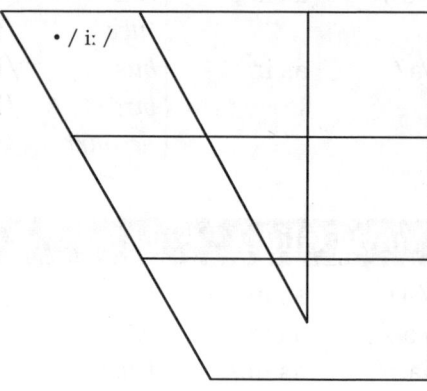

Fig. 3 / iː /

5.4.1 / iː / as in *these*.

The position of the highest point of the tongue for this vowel is indicated in the diagram. The front of the tongue is raised to a height just below the 'close' position: the lips are spread and the tongue is tense. The vowel is comparatively long, but the length is reduced before voiceless consonants.

The various spellings[2] for this vowel are:
- *e*, accented, generally *e* + consonant letter + mute *e*.

---

[2] The information about spellings is based on a frequency count undertaken by Mr. A.W.J. Barron at the English and Foreign Languages University (earlier known as Central Institute of English, Hyderabad). The spellings are given here in descending order of frequency in R.P.

The Sounds of English—Vowels

	British R.P.	Indian English Variant	Recommended Form
complete	/kəmˈpliːt/		
even	/ˈiːvᵊn/	[ˈiːʋən]	[ˈiːvən]
immediate	/ɪˈmiːdjət/	[ɪmmiːdɪet]³	[ɪˈmiːdjət]⁴
these	/ðiːz/	[d̪iːz]	[ðiːz]
♦ ee			
cheese	/tʃiːz/		
feed	/fiːd/		
green	/griːn/		
tree	/triː/		
♦ ea			
cream	/kriːm/		
dream	/driːm/		
each	/iːtʃ/		
lead	/liːd/		
reach	/riːtʃ/		
sea	/siː/		
teach	/tiːtʃ/		
♦ ie			
chief	/tʃiːf/		
field	/fiːld/		
piece	/piːs/		
♦ ei			
deceive	/dɪˈsiːv/	[dlsiːv]	[drˈsiːv]
receive	/rɪˈsiːv/	[rɪˈsiːv]	[rɪˈsiːv]
seize	/siːz/		
♦ i			
machine	/məˈʃiːn/		

³ The patterns of word accent in Indian English are not regular. Accent has not therefore been marked in every case.
⁴ Note the reduced length of [e].

police	/pəˈliːs/	[ˈpulɪs] or [poːlɪs]	[pʊˈliːs]

- Other spellings

key	/kiː/
people	/ˈpiːpəl/

Some Assamese, Bengali, Bihari Hindi, Gujarati, Marathi, and Odiya speakers in India do not always maintain the distinction between /iː/ and /ɪ/. They replace /iː/ by /ɪ/ and thus cannot distinguish between pairs like the following:

/iː/	/ɪ/
eat	*it*
feel	*fill*
field	*filled*
sleep	*slip*

It is necessary to keep the two phonemes separate and maintain the difference of quality. It is also necessary to give /iː/ adequate length.

5.4.2 /ɪ/ **as in** *bit*

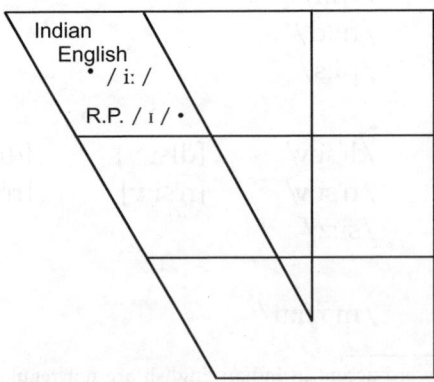

Fig. 4 /ɪ/

In the production of this vowel the hinder part of the front of the tongue is raised to a position between close and half-close.

In British R.P. /ɪ/ is a very common vowel in unaccented syllables, but the tendency in Indian English is to use the vowel suggested by the spelling

Spellings

	British R.P.	Indian English Variant	Recommended Form
♦ *i*			
bit	/bɪt/		
cliff	/klɪf/		
ink	/ɪŋk/		
rich	/rɪtʃ/		
silk	/sɪlk/		
thick	/θɪk/	[t̪ʰɪk/	[θɪk]
whip	/wɪp/	[ʋʰɪp]	[wɪp]

♦ *e*, unaccented. (Indian English has /ɛ/ instead of /ɪ/ in many of these words.)

begin	/bɪˈgɪn/	[bɪgˈɪn]	[bɪˈgɪn]
biggest	/ˈbɪgɪst/	[ˈbɪgɛst]	
careless	/ˈkɛəlɪs/	[ˈkeərlɛs]	
depend	/dɪˈpend/	[dɪˈpɛnd]	[dɪˈpɛnd]
effect	/ɪˈfekt/	[ɪfɛkt]	[ɪˈfɛkt]
goodness	/ˈgʊdnɪs/	[ˈgʊdnɛs]	
houses	/ˈhaʊzɪz/	[ˈhaʊsɛz]	[ˈhaʊzɪz]
matches	/ˈmætʃɪz/	[ˈmætʃɛz]	
neglect	/nɪˈglekt/	[nɛˈglɛkt]	[nɪˈglɛkt]
object (n.)	{/ˈɒbdʒɪkt/ /ˈɒbdʒekt/}	[ˈɒbdʒɛkt]	
perfect (adj.)	/ˈpɜːfɪkt/	[ˈpərfɛkt]	

	British R.P.	Indian English Variant	Recommended Form
reduce	/rɪˈdjuːs/	[rɪdjuːs]	[rɪˈdjuːs]
subject (n.)	/ˈsʌbdʒɪkt/ /ˈsʌbdʒekt/	[ˈsəbdʒɛkt]	
ticket	/ˈtɪkɪt/	[ˈtɪkɛt]	
useless	/ˈjuːslɪs/	[ˈjuːzlɛs]	[ˈjuːslɛs]
wanted	/ˈwɒntɪd/	[ˈʋaːntɛd]	[ˈwɒntɛd]

♦ *y*, medial and final:

city	/ˈsɪti/	[ˈsɪti]
mystery	/ˈmɪstəri/	[ˈmɪstəri]
system	/ˈsɪstɪm/	[ˈsɪstəm]

♦ *a*, unaccented. (Indian English has [e] instead of /ɪ/.)

baggage	/ˈbægɪdʒ/	[ˈbægedʒ]	
private	/ˈpraɪvɪt/	[ˈpraɪʋet]	
surface	/ˈsɜːfɪs/	[ˈsərfes]	
village	/ˈvɪlɪdʒ/	[ˈʋɪledʒ]	[ˈvɪledʒ]

♦ *ie* (Indian English has /iː/ instead of /ɪ/.)

carries	/ˈkæriz/	[ˈkæriːz]	[ˈkæriz]
handkerchief	/ˈhæŋkətʃɪf/	[ˈhæŋkərtʃiːf]	[ˈhæŋkətʃɪf]
parties	/ˈpɑːtɪz/	[ˈpɑːrtiːz]	[ˈpɑːrtɪz]

♦ Other spellings

busy	/ˈbɪzi/	[ˈbɪzi]	
minute	/ˈmɪnɪt/	[ˈmɪnət]	[ˈmɪnɪt]
coffee	/ˈkɒfi/	[ˈkɒfi]	
money	/ˈmʌni/	[ˈməni]	
carriage	/ˈkærɪdʒ/		
marriage	/ˈmærɪdʒ/		
bargain	/ˈbɑːɡɪn/	[ˈbɑːrɡen]	

	British R.P.	Indian English Variant	Recommended Form
captain	/ˈkæptɪn/	[ˈkæpten]	
mountain	/ˈmaʊntɪn/	[ˈmaʊnten]	
build	/bɪld/		
guilty	/ˈgɪlti/	[ˈgɪlti]	
James'	/ˈdʒeɪmzɪz/	[ˈdʒeːmsɛz]	[ˈdʒeːmzɛz]
foreign	/ˈfɒrən/ /ˈfɒrɪn/		

Some Assamese, Bengali, Bihari Hindi and Odiya speakers in India tend to replace /ɪ/ by a closer vowel [i], particularly in accented syllables. The result is that the distinction between pairs like the following is not always maintained:

/ɪ/	/iː/
bid	bead
hills	heels
live	leave

It is necessary to maintain the difference in quality between these two vowels. [i] can be changed to /ɪ/ by opening the mouth a little wider and producing the sound in a lax way.

5.4.3 Indian English /eː/ British R.P. /eɪ/ as in gate

In Indian English this vowel is a monophthong /eː/ — a centralised front, nearly half-close vowel. In British R.P. it is a diphthong /eɪ/, beginning slightly below the half-close position and moving towards R.P. /ɪ/. The lips are spread.

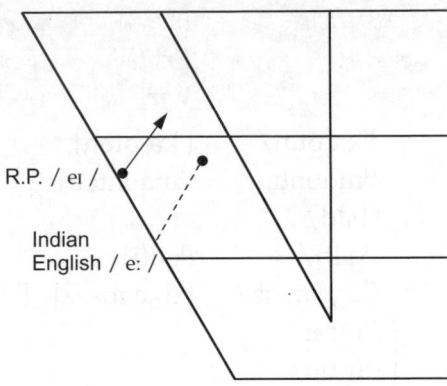

Fig. 5 / e /, / eɪ /

Spellings

♦ *a*, accented; generally *a* + consonant letter + mute *e*

	British R.P.	Indian English	Recommended Form
age	/eɪdʒ/	[e:dʒ]	
base	/beɪs/	[be:s]	
date	/deɪt/	[de:t]	
face	/feɪs/	[fe:s]	
gate	/geɪt/	[ge:t]	
hate	/heɪt/	[he:t]	
late	/leɪt/	[le:t]	
make	/meɪk/	[me:k]	
paste	/peɪst/	[pe:st]	
rate	/reɪt/	[re:t]	
state	/steɪt/	[ste:t]	
waste	/weɪst/	[ʊe:st]	[we:st]

♦ *ay*

| day | /deɪ/ | [de:] | |
| may | /meɪ/ | [me:] | |

	British R.P.	Indian English	Recommended Form
say	/seɪ/	[se:]	
pray	/preɪ/	[pre:]	
way	/weɪ/	[ʊe:]	[we:]

♦ ai

	British R.P.	Indian English	Recommended Form
aim	/eɪm/	[e:m]	
pain	/peɪn/	[pə:n]	
rain	/reɪn/	[re:n]	
straight	/streɪt/	[stre:t]	
wait	/weɪt/	[ʊe:t]	[we:t]

♦ ei, ey

	British R.P.	Indian English	Recommended Form
eight	/eɪt/	[e:t]	
grey	/greɪ/	[gre:]	
they	/ðeɪ/	[d̪e:]	[ðe:]
veil	/veɪl/	[ʊe:l]	[ve:l]
weigh	/weɪ/	[ʊe:]	[we:]

♦ ea

	British R.P.	Indian English	Recommended Form
break	/breɪk/	[brɛk]	[bre:k]
great	/greɪt/	[gre:t]	

Some Bengali, Bihari Hindi and Punjabi speakers in India tend to replace /e:/ by /ɛ/ or [ɛ:] and thus the distinction between pairs like the following is lost:

/e:/	/ɛ/
gate	get
later	letter
main	men

It is necessary to maintain this distinction and to give the monophthong /e:/ adequate length

5.4.4 British R.P. /e/ Indian English /ɛ/ as in *bed*

The quality of this vowel in Indian English is more open than in British R.P. In either case the front of the tongue is raised to a position between half-close and half-open. The lips are loosely spread. This vowel does not occur in the final position.

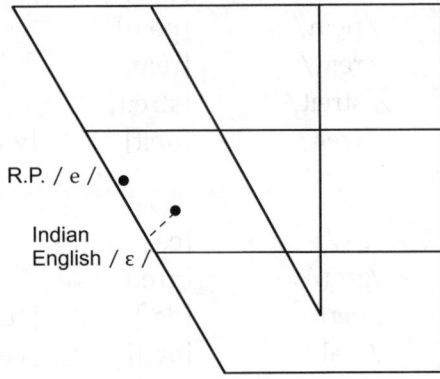

Fig. 6 / e /, / ɛ /

Spellings

♦ *e*, usually accented.

	British R.P.	Indian English	Recommended Form
bed	/bed/	[bɛd]	
left	/left/	[lɛft]	
melt	/melt/	[mɛlt]	
nest	/nest/	[nɛst]	
rest	/rest/	[rɛst]	
set	/set/	[sɛt]	
wet	/wet/	[ʊɛt]	[wɛt]
breath	/breθ/	[brɛtʰ]	[brɛθ]

	British R.P.	Indian English	Recommended Form
♦ ea			
dead	/ded/	[dɛd]	
feather	/ˈfeðə/	[ˈfeḏer]	[ˈfɛðər]
head	/hed/	[hɛd]	
jealous	/ˈdʒeləs/	[ˈdʒɛləs]	
lead (metal)	/led/	[lɛd]	
measure	/ˈmeʒə/	[ˈmɛʒər]	
pleasant	/ˈpleznt/	[ˈplɛzent]	
ready	/redi/	[ˈrɛdi]	
weather	/ˈweðə/	[ʋɛḏər]	[ˈwɛðər]
♦ a			
any	/ˈeni/	[ˈɛni]	
many	/ˈmeni/	[ˈmæni]	
♦ Other spellings			
bury	/ˈberi/	[ˈbəri]	[ˈbɛri]
friend	/frend/	[frɛnd]	
leisure	/ˈleʒə/	[ˈlɛʒər]	
said	/sed/	[sɛd]	

Many speakers in India replace the vowel /e/ by the Indian [ɛ] or [eː], with the result that pairs like the following are not distinguished:

Indian /ɛ/ R.P. /e/	Indian /eː/ R.P. /eɪ/
fell	fail
let	late
test	taste
met	mate
west	waste

tell   *tale*

Indian [e:] can be changed to /ɛ/ by opening the mouth a little wider.

Some Hindi and Punjabi speakers replace /ɛ/ by /æ/; this leads to confusion between pairs like *bed* and *bad*. /æ/ can be changed to /ɛ/ by closing the mouth a little.

5.4.5 /æ/ as in *bad*

For this vowel the front of the tongue is slightly below the half open position and the lips are in the neutral position. /æ/ does not occur finally.

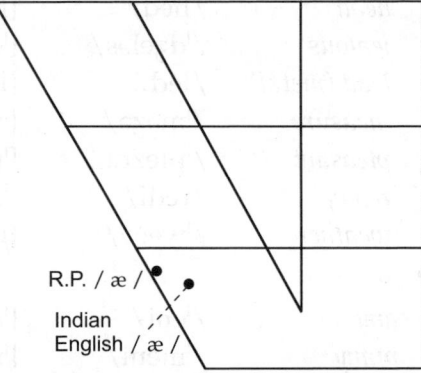

Fig. 7   / æ /

Spelling

* a

bad	/bæd/
fan	/fæn/
hat	/hæt/
mass	/mæs/
rank	/ræŋk/
sad	/sæd/
tax	/tæks/

Some Assamese, Bengali and Hindi speakers replace /æ/ by /ɛ/, with the result that there is confusion between pairs like the following:

| /æ/ | Indian English / ɛ / |
| | British R.P: / e / |

band	bend
man	men
sad	said

/ ɛ / can be changed to / æ / by opening the mouth wider.

5.4.6. British R.P.   /ʌ/ ⎫
Indian English /ə/ ⎬ as in *bus*
⎭

British R.P. /ʌ/ is a central vowel, between open and half-open; the lips are neutral. This vowel does not occur finally.

In R.P., /ʌ/, /ɜː/ and /ə/ are separate phonemes, but corresponding to these, Indian English has only one phoneme /ə/, realised as [ə] and [ʌ], the two being used indiscriminately.

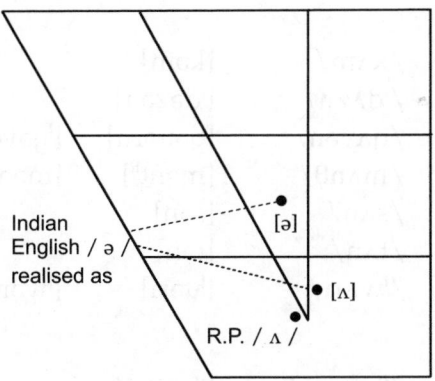

Fig. 8 R.P. / ʌ / Indian English / ə /

Spellings

	British R.P.	Indian English	Recommended Form
♦ *u*			
bundle	/ˈbʌndl/	[ˈbəndl]	
cup	/kʌp/	[kəp]	
dust	/dʌst/	[dəst]	
gun	/gʌn/	[gən]	
hunt	/hʌnt/	[hənt]	
much	/mʌtʃ/	[mətʃ]	
pump	/pʌmp/	[pəmp]	
run	/rʌn/	[rən]	
such	/sʌtʃ/	[sətʃ]	
thus	/ðʌs/	[d̪əs]	[ðəs]
uncle	/ˈʌŋkl/	[ˈəŋkl]	
♦ *o*			
come	/kʌm/	[kəm]	
dozen	/ˈdʌzn/	[ˈdəzən]	
govern	/gʌvən/	[gəʋərn]	[ˈgəvərn]
month	/mʌnθ/	[mənt̪ʰ]	[mənθ]
son	/sʌn/	[sən]	
ton	/tʌn/	[tən]	
worry	/ˈwʌri/	[ˈʋəri]	[ˈwəri]
♦ *ou*			
country	/ˈkʌntri/	[ˈkəntri]	
double	/ˈdʌbəl/	[ˈdəbəl]	
enough	/ɪˈnʌf/	[ɛnəf]	[ɪˈnəf]
rough	/rʌf/	[rəf]	
trouble	/ˈtrʌbəl/	[ˈtrəbəl]	
young	/jʌŋ/	[jəŋ]	

- Other spellings

  blood   /blʌd/   [bləd]
  does   /dʌz/   [dəz]

Many Indian speakers often use [ə], a central vowel, instead of a more open variety [ʌ], even in stressed syllables, where R.P. has [ʌ]. The distribution of [ʌ] and [ə] in Indian English is not governed by any well established pattern. The two vowels may therefore be treated as free variants, and grouped under one phoneme symbolised as /ə/.

5.4.7 Indian English /aː/   British R.P. /ɑː/   as in *card*

This is a long vowel produced with the mouth wide open. The quality in Indian English is somewhat centralised compared to the R.P. vowel, which is back and fully open.

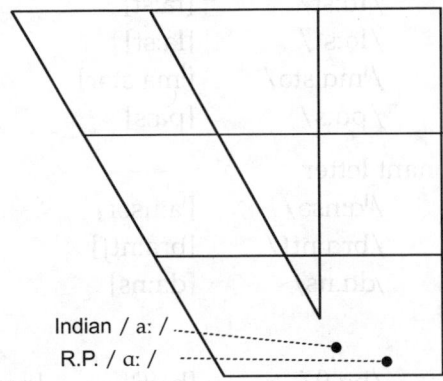

Fig. 9   / aː /, / ɑː /

Spellings

	British R.P.	Indian English	Recommended Form
♦ *ar* + consonant letter; *ar-* final.			
art	/ɑːt/[5]	[aːrt]	
bar	/bɑː/	[baːr]	
card	/kɑːd/	[kaːrd]	
farm	/fɑːm/	[faːrm]	
hard	/hɑːd/	[haːrd]	
large	/lɑːdʒ/	[laːrdʒ]	
march	/mɑːtʃ/	[maːrtʃ]	
part	/pɑːt/	[paːrt]	
♦ *as* + consonant letter			
ask	/ɑːsk/	[aːsk]	
basket	/ˈbɑːskɪt/	[ˈbaːskɛt]	
castle	/ˈkɑːsl/	[ˈkaːsl]	
fast	/fɑːst/	[faːst]	
last	/lɑːst/	[laːst]	
master	/ˈmɑːstə/	[ˈmaːstər]	
pass	/pɑːs/	[paːs]	
♦ *an* + consonant letter			
answer	/ˈɑːnsə/	[ˈaːnsər]	
branch	/brɑːntʃ/	[braːntʃ]	
dance	/dɑːns/	[daːns]	
♦ *ath* final			
bath	/bɑːθ/	[baːt̪ʰ]	[baːθ]
path	/pɑːθ/	[paːt̪ʰ]	[paːθ]

---

[5]In British R.P. / r / occurs only before vowels.

	British R.P.	Indian English	Recommended Form

- *af* + consonant letter

  after /ˈɑːftə/ [ˈɑːfter]

  staff /stɑːf/ [stɑːf]

- *al* + consonant letter

  calm /kɑːm/ [kɑːm]

  half /hɑːf/ [hɑːf]

- *au*

  aunt /ɑːnt/ [ɑːnt]

  laugh /lɑːf/ [lɑːf]

- *a*

  drama /ˈdrɑːmə/ [ˈdrɑːma]

  father /ˈfɑːðə/ [ˈfɑːd̪ər] [ˈfɑːðər]

  rather /ˈrɑːðə/ [ˈrɑːd̪ər] [ˈrɑːðər]

- *-er* + consonant letter

  clerk /klɑːk/ [klərk] [klɑːrk]

- *-ear* + consonant letter

  heart /hɑːt/ [hɑːrt]

Some Telugu speakers replace /ɑː/ by [ɒː] or [ɒ] with the result that there is confusion between pairs like the following:

Indian English /ɑː/ R.P. /ɑː/	/ɒ/
last	lost
laughed	loft
cart	cot
heart	hot

There should be no rounding of lips for /aː/, and the retention of /r/ in all positions would help to maintain some of the contrasts.

Some Telugu and Malayalam speakers replace /aː/ by /æ/ in words like *class* and *plant*.

5.4.8 /ɒ/ as in *hot*.

/ɒ/ is a back vowel, fully open in British R.P. and slightly raised in Indian English, articulated with rounded lips. The R.P. vowel is short; in Indian English the length varies. In R.P. /ɒ/ does not occur finally.

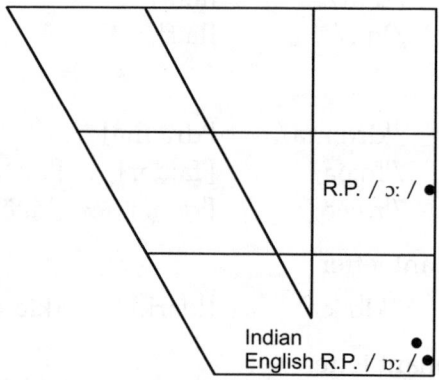

Fig. 10 / ɒ /, / ɔː /

Spellings	British R.P.	Indian English	Recommended Form
♦ o			
bottle	/ˈbɒtᵊl/		
dog	/dɒg/		
fond	/fɒnd/		
God	/gɒd/		

The Sounds of English—Vowels

	British R.P.	Indian English	Recommended Form
hot	/hɒt/		
lock	/lɒk/		
not	/nɒt/		
off	/ɒf/		
pot	/pot/		
rob	/rɒb/		
solve	/sɒlv/	[sɒlʊ]	[sɒlv]

- ♦ -or accented + vowel letter

borrow	/ˈbɒrəʊ/	[ˈbɒroː]	
moral	/ˈmɒrəl/		
sorry	/ˈsɒri/		

- ♦ /w/ + a + consonant (Indian English has /aː/ [a] in these words.)

| quality | /ˈkwɒləti/ /ˈkwɒlɪti/ | [ˈkwalɪti] | [ˈkwɒlɪti] |
| want | /wɒnt/ | [ʊɒnt] | [wɒnt] |

- ♦ au

| because | /bɪˈkɒz/ | | |

- ♦ ou

| cough | /kɒf/ | [kəf] | [kɒf] |

- ♦ Other spellings

gone	/gɒn/		
shone	/ʃɒn/	[ʃoːn]	[ʃɒn]
knowledge	/ˈnɒlɪdʒ/		

Some Indian speakers replace /ɒ/ by [a] in words spelt *wa-*. [a] can be changed to /ɒ/ by a slight rounding of the lips.

5.4.9 British R.P. /ɔː/ as in $\begin{cases} all \\ horse \\ force \end{cases}$

Indian English [ɒː] as in *all*, /ɒr/ as in *horse*, and /oːr/ as in *force*.

British R.P. /ɔː/ is produced by raising the back of the tongue to a position between half-open and half-close. (See Fig. 10.) The lips are rounded. It is a long vowel but the length is reduced before voiceless consonants.

The distinction between /ɒ/ and /ɔː/ is not observed in Indian English, [ɒː], /ɒr/ or /oːr/ being used in place of /ɔː/.

Spellings

	British R.P.	Indian English	Recommended Form
♦ **all**			
all	/ɔːl/	[ɒːl]	
ball	/bɔːl/	[bɒːl]	
call	/kɔːl/	[kɒːl]	
fall	/fɔːl/	[fɒːl]	
hall	/hɔːl/	[hɒːl]	
wall	/wɔːl/	[wɒːl]	
♦ **or + consonant letter**			
corn	/kɔːn/	[kɒrn]	
horse	/hɔːs/	[hɒrs]	
morning	/ˈmɔːnɪŋ/	[ˈmɒrnɪŋ]	
north	/nɔːθ/	[nɒrt̪ʰ]	[nɒrθ]
force	/fɔːs/	[foːrs]	
♦ **our**			
court	/kɔːt/	[koːrt]	

The Sounds of English—Vowels

	British R.P.	Indian English	Recommended Form
four	/fɔː/	[foːr]	
pour	/pɔː/	[poːr]	
♦ or final			
nor	/nɔː/	[nɒːr]	
♦ ore			
before	/bɪfɔː/	[bɪˈfoːr]	
more	/mɔː/	[moːr]	
sore	/sɔː/	[soːr]	
tore	/tɔː/	[toːr]	
♦ ough +t			
bought	/bɔːt/	[bɒːt]	
fought	/fɔːt/	[fɒːt]	
thought	/θɔːt/	[t̪ʰɒːt]	[θɒːt]
♦ oor			
door	/dɔː/	[doːr]	
floor	/flɔː/	[floːr]	
♦ aw			
awkward	/ˈɔːkwəd/	[ˈɒːkwərd]	
law	/lɔː/	[lɒː]	
saw	/sɔː/	[sɒː]	
♦ au			
cause	/kɔːz/	[kɒːz]	
fault	/fɔːlt/	[fɒlt]	
♦ al+k			
chalk	/tʃɔːk/	[tʃɒːk]	
talk	/tɔːk/	[tɒːk]	
walk	/wɔːk/	[wɒːk]	

♦ /w/ + *ar* + consonant letter (Indian English generally has /aː/ in these words).

	British R.P.	Indian English	Recommended Form
quarter	/ˈkwɔːtə/	[ˈkwaːrtər]	[ˈkwɒrtər]
towards	/təˈwɔːdz/ /tʊˈwɔːdz/	[tʊwərdz]	[tʊˈwɒrdz]
warm	/wɔːm/	[ʋaːrm]	[wɒrm]

♦ *oar*
| *board* | /bɔːd/ | [boːrd] | |

♦ *augh + t*
| *caught* | /kɔːt/ | [kɒt] | |
| *daughter* | /ˈdɔːtər/ | [ˈdɒːtər] | |

♦ Other spellings
broad	/brɔːd/	[brɒːd]	
story	/ˈstɔːrɪ/	[ˈstoːrɪ]	
war	/wɔː/	[ʋaːr]	[wɒːr]

Most Indian speakers use [ɒː] or [ɒ] in words like *all, brought, saw* and *talk*. It is desirable to give the vowel sufficient length in such words.

Most Indian speakers use /ɒr/ in words like *born, form, north, order* and *short*, and /oːr/ in words like *before, course, four, more, restore* and *store*. It is necessary to retain /r/ after the vowel in such words if /ɔː/ is not used.

5.4.10 Indian English /oː/ ⎫
British R.P. /əʊ/ ⎬ as in *home*

In British R.P. this vowel is a diphthong, beginning at a central position just below half-close and moving in the direction of /ʊ/. The lips are neutral in the beginning and rounded towards the end. In Indian English a monophthong /oː/ is used.

The Sounds of English—Vowels

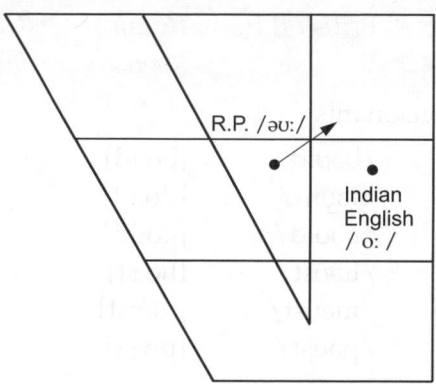

Fig. 11. / oː /, / əʊ /

Spellings

	British R.P.	Indian English	Recommended Form

- *o* alone
  - *o* + consonant letter + mute *e*
bone	/bəʊn/	[boːn]	
home	/həʊm/	[hoːm]	
nose	/nəʊz/	[noːz]	
rope	/rəʊp/	[roːp]	

  - *o* in other accented positions
both	/bəʊθ/	[boːt̪ʰ]	[boːθ]
open	/ˈəʊpən/	[ˈoːpən]	
social	/ˈsəʊʃəl/	[ˈsoːʃəl]	

  - *o* final
go	/gəʊ/	[goː]	
no	/nəʊ/	[noː]	
so	/səʊ/	[soː]	

	British R.P.	Indian English	Recommended Form

- o + two consonants

bold	/bəʊld/	[boːld]	
don't	/dəʊnt/	[doːnt]	
gold	/gəʊld/	[goːld]	
host	/həʊst/	[hoːst]	
most	/məʊst/	[moːst]	
post	/pəʊst/	[poːst]	

- oll

roll	/rəʊl/	[roːl]	

- ow

blow	/bləʊ/	[bloː]	
flow	/fləʊ/	[floː]	
know	/nəʊ/	[noː]	
narrow	/ˈnærəʊ/	[ˈnæroː]	
sow	/səʊ/	[soː]	
window	/ˈwɪndəʊ/	[ˈʊɪndoː]	[ˈwɪndoː]

- oa

boat	/bəʊt/	[boːt]	
coast	/kəʊst/	[koːst]	
load	/ləʊd/	[loːd]	
road	/rəʊd/	[roːd]	
soap	/səʊp/	[soːp]	

- ou

shoulder	/ˈʃəʊldə/	[ˈʃoːldər]	
though	/ðəʊ/	[d̪oː]	[ðoː]

5.4.11 /ʊ/ as in *book*

In the production of this vowel the back of the tongue is raised to a position between close and half-close. The lips are closely but loosely rounded and the tongue is lax.

In Indian English the vowel is closer than in R.P.

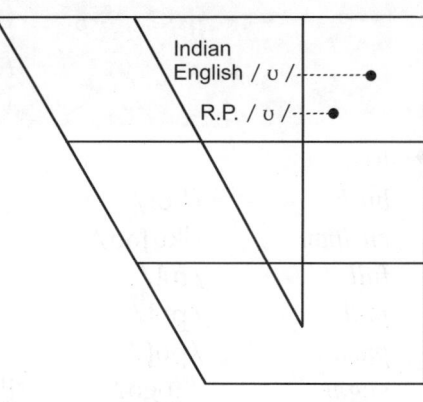

Fig. 12. / ʊ /

/ʊ/ does not occur at the beginning of words. Finally it occurs only in the weak from of the word *to*.

Spellings

	British R.P.	Indian English Variant	Recommended Form
♦ *oo*, generally followed by *k*			
book	/bʊk/		
cook	/kʊk/		
foot	/fʊt/		
good	/gʊd/		
hook	/hʊk/		
look	/lʊk/		
took	/tʊk/		
wood	/wʊd/		
♦ *o*			
woman	/ˈwʊmən/	[ˈwomən]	[ˈwʊmən]

42 SPOKEN ENGLISH

	British R.P.	Indian English Variant	Recommended Form
◆ u			
bush	/bʊʃ/		
cushion	/ˈkʊʃən/		
full	/fʊl/		
pull	/pʊl/		
push	/pʊʃ/		
sugar	/ˈʃʊgə/	[ˈʃʊgər]	
◆ oul			
could	/kʊd/		
should	/ʃʊd/		
would	/wʊd/		

Some Bengali speakers replace /ʊ/ by a closer vowel [u]. This leads to confusion between pairs like *full* and *fool*. [u] can be changed to /ʊ/ by opening the mouth a little wider.

5.4.12 /u:/ as in *rule, tube*

This is a long back close vowel. The lips are closely rounded and the tongue is tense. The length is reduced before voiceless consonants.

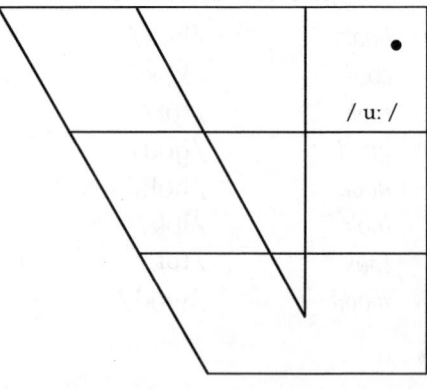

Fig. 13. / u: /

Spellings

- *u*, either alone in an accented syllable or followed by a consonant letter and mute *e*. (often pronounced /juː/ when initial, or after a plosive, a nasal, or /f, v, h/)

	British R.P.	Indian English Variant	Recommended Form
duty	/ˈdjuːti/		
funeral	/ˈfjuːnərəl/		
music	/ˈmjuːzɪk/		
pupil	{/ˈpjuːpᵊl/ /ˈpjuːpɪl/		
rude	/ruːd/		
tube	/tjuːb/		
union	/ˈjuːnjən/	[ˈjuːnɪən]	

- *oo* + consonant letter

choose	/tʃuːz/		
food	/fuːd/		
loose	/luːs/		
moon	/muːn/		
noon	/nuːn/		
soon	/suːn/		
tool	/tuːl/		
tooth	/tuːθ/	[tuːt̪ʰ]	[tuːθ]

- *o*

do	/duː/		
lose	/luːz/		
move	/muːv/	[muːʊ]	[muːv]
who	/huː/		

- *ou*

group	/gruːp/	[grʊp]	[gruːp]

	British R.P.	Indian English Variant	Recommended Form
soup	/su:p/		
through	/θru:/	[t̪ʰru:]	[θru:]
wound	/wu:nd/		
you	/ju:/		

- ui

fruit	/fru:t/		
juice	/dʒu:s/	[dʒju:s]	[dʒu:s]
nuisance	/ˈnju:sᵊns/	[ˈnuɪsɛns]	[ˈnju:səns]
suit	/su:t/ /sju:t/		

- ew

new	/nju:/	

- Other spellings

beauty	/ˈbju:ti/	
shoe	/ʃu:/	
two	/tu:/	

Some Bengali and Bihari Hindi speakers replace /u:/ by [ʊ]

This leads to confusion between pairs like *fool* and *full*. [ʊ] can be changed to /u:/ by closing the mouth a little and making the vowel longer.

5.4.13 British R.P. /ɜː/ </br>Indian English /ər/ } as in *serve*.

British R.P. /ɜː/ is a central vowel between half-close and half-open, the lips being neutral. It occurs only in accented syllables. It is a long vowel, but the length is reduced before voiceless consonants. In Indian English it is replaced by [ər] or [ʌr].

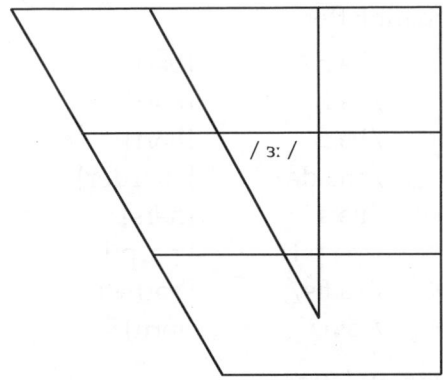

Fig. 14   R.P. / ɜː /

Spellings

	British R.P.	Indian English Variant	Recommended Form
♦ *er* + consonant letter			
perfect (adj.)	/ˈpɜːfɪkt/	[ˈpərfɛkt]	
serve	/sɜːv/	[sərʊ]	[sərv]
term	/tɜːm/	[tərm]	
♦ *ir* + consonant letter			
bird	/bɜːd/	[bərd]	

	British R.P.	Indian English Variant	Recommended Form
circle	/ˈsɜːkᵊl/	[ˈsərkᵊl]	
dirt	/dɜːt/	[dərt]	
firm	/fɜːm/	[fərm]	
girl	/gɜːl/	[gərl]	
thirst	/θɜːst/	[t̪ʰərst]	[θərst]

♦ *ur* + consonant letter

	British R.P.	Indian English Variant
burn	/bɜːn/	[bərn]
curl	/kɜːl/	[kərl]
hurt	/hɜːt/	[hərt]
murder	/ˈmɜːdə/	[ˈmərder]
nurse	/nɜːs/	[nərs]
purple	/ˈpɜːpᵊl/	[ˈpərpᵊl]
surface	/ˈsɜːfɪs/	[ˈsərfes]
turn	/tɜːn/	[tərn]

♦ *wor* + consonant letter

	British R.P.	Indian English Variant	Recommended Form
word	/wɜːd/	[ʊərd]	[wərd]

♦ *ear* + consonant letter

	British R.P.	Indian English Variant
early	/ˈɜːlɪ/	[ˈərlɪ]
heard	/hɜːd/	[hərd]
learn	/lɜːn/	[lərn]
search	/sɜːtʃ/	[sərtʃ]

♦ *our* + consonant letter

	British R.P.	Indian English Variant
journey	/ˈdʒɜːnɪ/	[ˈdʒərnɪ]

Most Indian speakers use [ər] or [ʌr] in place of R.P. /ɜː/. It is necessary to retain /r/ after the vowel if /ɜː/ is not used.

The Sounds of English—Vowels

5.4.14. /ə/ as in } *account* **(first syllable)**
human **(second syllable)**

/ə:/ is a central vowel with neutral lip position. In British R.P. the tongue-raising is between half-open and half-close in the non-final position and nearly half-open in the final position.

In R.P. /ə/ is a very frequent vowel, occurring only in unaccented syllables. In Indian English, instead of /ə/ the vowel indicated by the spelling is generally used. [ə] and [ʌ] are free variants in Indian English.

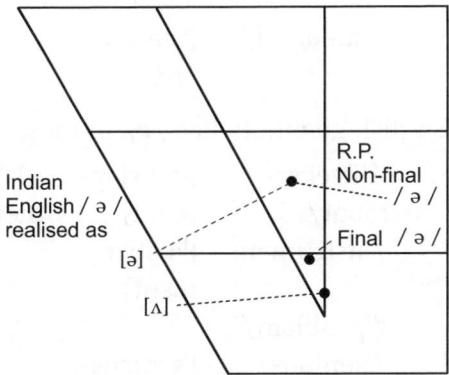

Fig. 15 R.P. / ə /

Spellings

Initial and medial /ə/

	British R.P.	Indian English Variant	Recommended Form
♦ a (Indian English does not always use /ə/ in these words.)			
about	/əˈbɑʊt/	[əˈbaʊt]	
breakfast	/ˈbrekfəst/	[ˈbrɛkfast]	

	British R.P.	Indian English Variant	Recommended Form
gentleman	/ˈdʒentlmən/	[ˈdʒentlmæn]	
human	/ˈhjuːmən/		
substance	/ˈsʌbstəns/	[ˈsəbstɛns]	

♦ **ar**

	British R.P.	Indian English Variant	Recommended Form
backward	/ˈbækwəd/	[bækwərd]	
particular	/pəˈtikjʊlə/	[pərtɪkjʊlər]	[pərˈtɪkʊlər]
standard	/ˈstændəd/	[ˈstændərd]	

♦ ɛ (Indian English generally has /ɛ/ in these words.)

	British R.P.	Indian English Variant	Recommended Form
development	/diˈveləpmənt/	[dɛvɛləpment]	[dɛˈvɛləpment]
instrument	/ɪnstrumənt/	[ˈinstrumɛnt]	
problem	/ˈprɒbləm/		
sentence	/ˈsentəns/	[ˈsɛntɛns]	

♦ **er**

	British R.P.	Indian English Variant	Recommended Form
entertain	/entəˈteɪn/	[ɛntərteːn]	[ɛntərˈteːn]
liberty	/ˈlɪbətɪ/	[ˈlɪbarti]	
otherwise	/ʌðəwaɪz/	[ˈədərʊaɪz]	[ˈəðarwaɪz]

♦ **i**

	British R.P.	Indian English Variant	Recommended Form
terrible	/ˈterəbl/	[ˈtɛrɪbəl]	

♦ **o**

	British R.P.	Indian English Variant	Recommended Form
condition	/kənˈdɪʃən/	[kəndɪʃən]	[kənˈdɪʃən]
factory	/ˈfæktᵊri/		
observe	/əbˈzɜːv/	[ɒbzəru]	[ɒbˈzərv]
produce (v.)	/prəˈdjuːs/	[prodjuːs]	[proˈdjuːs]

	British R.P.	Indian English Variant	Recommended Form
society	/sə'saɪətɪ/	[so'saɛtɪ]	

- *or*

effort	/'efət/	['ɛfərt]	

- *ou*

continuous	/kən'tɪnjʊəs/		
famous	/'feɪməs/	['fe:məs]	

- *u*

succeed	/sək'si:d/		

- *ur*

surprise	/sə'praɪz/	[sər'praɪz]	

Final /ə/

- *-a* (Indian English has /a/ in these words.)

drama	/'drɑ:mə/	['drɑ:ma]	
India	/'ɪndjə/	['ɪndɪa]	

- *-ar*

beggar	/'begə/	['bɛgər]	
collar	/'kɒlə/	['kɒlər]	
dollar	/'dɒlə/	['dɒlər]	

- *-er*

bigger	/'bɪgə/	['bɪgər]	
elder	/'eldə/	['ɛldər]	
father	/'fɑ:ðə/	['fɑ:d̪ər]	['fɑ:ðər]
hunger	/'hʌŋgə/	['həŋgər]	
order	/'ɔ:də/	['ɒrdər]	

- *-or*

actor	/'æktə/	['æktər]	

	British R.P.	Indian English Variant	Recommended Form
doctor	/ˈdɒktə/	[ˈdɒktər]	
motor	/ˈməʊtə/	[ˈmoːtər]	
sailor	/ˈseɪlə/	[ˈseːlər]	

♦ -*our*

	British R.P.	Indian English Variant	Recommended Form
colour	/ˈkʌlə/	[ˈkələr]	
favour	/ˈfeɪvə/	[ˈfeːʊər]	[ˈfeːvər]
honour	/ˈɒnə/	[ˈɒnər]	

♦ -*ough*

	British R.P.	Indian English Variant	Recommended Form
thorough	/ˈθʌrə/	[ˈt̪ʰɒro]	[ˈθɒro]

♦ -*ure*

	British R.P.	Indian English Variant	Recommended Form
creature	/ˈkriːtʃə/	[ˈkriːtʃər]	
measure	/ˈmeʒə/	[ˈmɛʒər]	
nature	/ˈneɪtʃə/	[ˈneːtʃər]	
picture	/ˈpɪktʃə/	[ˈpɪktʃər]	

♦ -*re*

	British R.P.	Indian English Variant	Recommended Form
centre	/ˈsentə/	[ˈsɛntər]	
theatre	/ˈθɪətə/	[ˈt̪ʰjeːter]	[θɪˈetər]

5.4.15 Diphthongs

Diphthongs are vowel glides within a syllable. For example, in a word of more than one syllable a glide would remain part of one syllable only. In the two-syllable word *flying* the first syllable has the diphthong / aɪ / and the second syllable has the pure vowel / ɪ /. On the other hand, in the phrase *draw it*, / ɔː / in *draw* and / ɪ / in *it* do not form a diphthong because they belong to two separate syllables. Again in the sentence *Shakespearean drama is really fascinating*, the vowel / ə /

in the second syllable of *drama* and the vowel / ɪ / in the word *is*, are not elements of a diphthong but two separate vowels because they belong to two separate syllables. In R.P. diphthongs most of the length and stress is given to the first element. These diphthongs are long vowels, but the length is reduced before voiceless consonants. The R.P. diphthongs /eɪ/ and /əʊ/ have already been discussed. The other diphthongs are described here.

5.4.16 /aɪ/ **as in** *bite*

In the production of /aɪ/ there is a glide from the front open position towards /ɪ/; the starting point is retracted in Indian English. The lips change from a neutral to a loosely spread position.

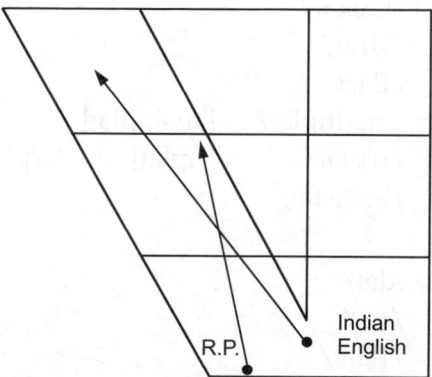

Fig. 16   R.P. / aɪ /

Spellings

♦ *i*, accented
  - *i* + consonant letter + mute *e*
    bite/baɪt/, fine/faɪn/, ice/aɪs/, mine/maɪn/, nice/naɪs/, pipe/paɪp/, ride/raɪd/, time/taɪm/, write/, raɪt/

	British R.P.	Indian English Variant	Recommended Form

- *i* in other positions
  - climb   /klaɪm/
  - rival   /ˈraɪvəl/   [ˈraɪʊəl]   [ˈraɪvəl]
  - silence /ˈsaɪləns/   [ˈsaɪlɛns]
  - tidy   /ˈtaɪdi/

- *y*, generally accented.
  - *y* + consonant letter + mute *e*
    - type   /taɪp/
  - *y* in other positions.
    - cry   /kraɪ/
    - cycle   /ˈsaɪkl/
               /ˈsaɪkəl/
    - dry   /ˈdraɪ/
    - fly   /flaɪ/
    - multiply /ˈmʌltɪplaɪ/   [ˈməltɪplaɪ]
    - reply   /rɪˈplaɪ/   [rɪplaɪ]   [rɪˈplaɪ]
    - satisfy /ˈsætɪsfaɪ/

- *ie*
  - die   /daɪ/
  - tie   /taɪ/
  - flies /flaɪz/
  - cried /kraɪd/

- *igh*
  - high   /haɪ/
  - light /laɪt/
  - might /maɪt/
  - fight /faɪt/
  - night /naɪt/
  - right /raɪt/
  - tight /taɪt/

	British R.P.	Indian English Variant	Recommended Form
♦ ei			
either	/ˈaɪðə/	[ˈaɪd̪ər]	[ˈaɪðər]
height	/haɪt/		
neither	/ˈnaɪðə/	[ˈnaɪd̪ər]	[ˈnaɪðər]
♦ Other spellings			
child	/tʃaɪld/		
kind	/kaɪnd/		
eye	/aɪ/		
buy	/baɪ/		
island	/ˈaɪlənd/	[ˈaɪlænd]	

In words like *fire*, *hire*, and *science*, R.P. has /aɪə/, but Indian English generally has [aɛr] in *fire* and *hire* and /aɪ/ in *science*.

5.4.17 /ɔɪ/ as in *boil*

In R.P. the glide for this diphthong begins near the back half-open position and moves in the direction of /ɪ/. In Indian

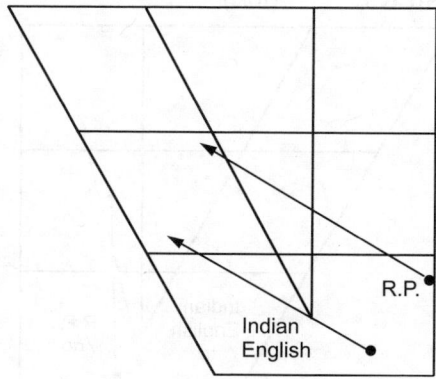

Fig. 17 R.P. / ɔɪ /

English it begins in a more open position. The lips are open-rounded at the beginning and neutral at the end.

Spellings

	British R.P.	Indian English Variant	Recommended Form
♦ *oi*			
boil	/bɔɪl/		
choice	/tʃɔɪs/		
noise	/nɔɪz/		
oil	/ɔɪl/		
point	/pɔɪnt/		
voice	/vɔɪs/	[ʊɔɪs]	[vɔɪs]
♦ *oy*			
annoy	/əˈnɔɪ/		
boy	/bɔɪ/		
toy	/tɔɪ/		

5.4.18.   Indian English /aʊ/
   British R.P.   /ɑʊ/   as in house

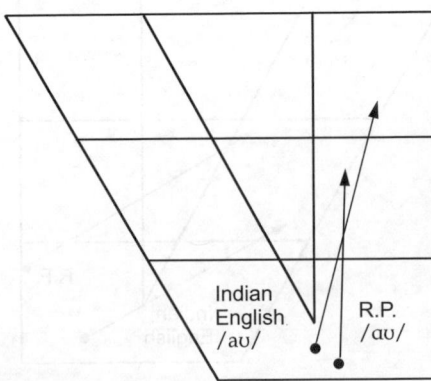

Fig. 18   / aʊ /, / ɑʊ /

The Sounds of English—Vowels

The glide for this diphthong begins between the front and the back open positions and proceeds in the direction of /ʊ/. The lips are neutral in the beginning and weakly rounded at the end.

Spellings

	British R.P.	Indian English Variant	Recommended Form
♦ *ou*			
about	/əˈbaʊt/	[əˈbaʊt]	
bound	/baʊnd/	[baʊnd]	
doubt	/daʊt/	[daʊt]	
house	/haʊs/	[haʊs]	
loud	/laʊd/	[laʊd]	
mouth	/maʊθ/	[maʊt̺ʰ]	[maʊθ]
out	/aʊt/	[aʊt]	
round	/raʊnd/	[raʊnd]	
sound	/saʊnd/	[saʊnd]	
♦ *ow*			
allow	/əˈlaʊ/	[ɛlaʊ]	[əˈlaʊ]
cow	/kaʊ/	[kaʊ]	
how	/haʊ/	[haʊ]	
now	/naʊ/	[naʊ]	
town	/taʊn/	[taʊn]	

In words like *our, sour, tower*, R.P. has /aʊə/, but Indian English generally has [aʊər] or [aːə] The latter is preferable.

5.4.19 /ɪə/ as in *cheer*

The glide for /ɪə/ begins with /ɪ/ and moves towards /ə/. The lips are neutral.

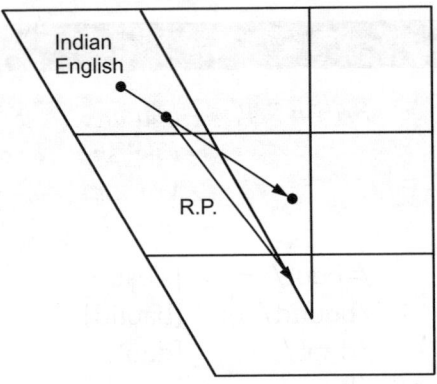

Fig. 19 / ɪə /

Spellings

Stressed /ɪə/

- *e*, stressed + *r* (Indian English has /iː/ in these words.)

	British R.P.	Indian English Variant	Recommended Form
period	/ˈpɪərɪəd/	[ˈpiːrɪəd]	
serious	/ˈsɪərɪəs/	[ˈsiːrɪəs]	
zero	/ˈzɪərəʊ/	[ˈziːroː]	

- *eer*

| cheer | /tʃɪə/ | [tʃɪər] |
| deer | /dɪə/ | [dɪər] |

The Sounds of English—Vowels

	British R.P.	Indian English Variant	Recommended Form
♦ ear			
dear	/dɪə/	[dɪər]	
ear	/ɪə/	[ɪər]	
fear	/fɪə/	[fɪər]	
hear	/hɪə/	[hɪər]	
near	/nɪə/	[nɪər]	
♦ ere			
here	/hɪə/	[hɪər]	
mere	/mɪə/	[mɪər]	
severe	/sɪˈvɪə/	[sɪˈʊɪər]	[sɪˈvɪər]
♦ ier			
fierce	/fɪəs/	[fɪərs]	
♦ ea			
idea	/aɪˈdɪə/	[aɪdɪa]	[aɪˈdɪa]
real	/rɪəl/		
theatre	/ˈθɪətə/	[t̪ʰjeːtər]	[θɪˈetər]

Unstressed /ɪə/ has the prominence on the second element.

Examples:

	British R.P.	Indian English Variant	Recommended Form
period	/ˈpɪərɪəd/	(second syllable)	[ˈpiːrɪəd]
serious	/ˈsɪərɪəs/	"	[ˈsiːərɪəs]

5.4.20 Indian English /eə/
British R.P. /ɛə/ } as in *air*

The glide for this diphthong begins between front half-close and half-open positions and moves towards /ə/. The lips are neutral.

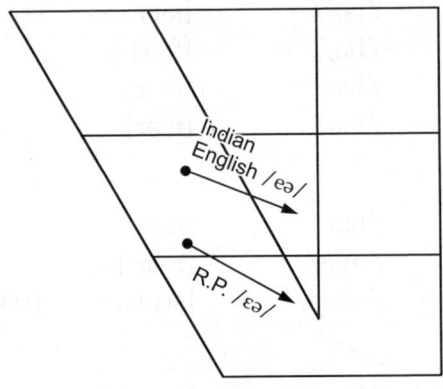

Fig. 20   /eə/, /ɛə/

Spellings

	British R.P.	Indian English Variant	Recommended Form
♦ *air*			
air	/ɛə/	[eər]	
chair	/tʃɛə/	[tʃeər]	
fair	/fɛə/	[feər]	
hair	/hɛə/	[heər]	
pair	/pɛə/	[peər]	
♦ *ar* accented + vowel letter			
bare	/bɛə/	[beər]	
care	/kɛə/	[keər]	

	British R.P.	Indian English Variant	Recommended Form
dare	/dɛə/	[deər]	
rare	/rɛə/	[reər]	
share	/ʃɛə/	[ʃeər]	
various	/ˈvɛərɪəs/	[ˈʊeːrɪəs]	[ˈveːrɪəs]

- ear

bear	/bɛə/	[beər]	
tear (v.)	/tɛə/	[teər]	
wear	/wɛə/	[ʊeər]	[weər]

- R.P. /eɪə/ reduced to /ɛə/

| prayer | /prɛə/ | [preər] | |

- Other spellings

aeroplane	/ˈɛərəpleɪn/	[ˈeːropleːn]	
their	/ðɛə/	[d̪eər]	[ðeər]

5.4.21 /ʊə/ as in *poor*

The glide for /ʊə/ is from /ʊ/ to /ə/. The lips are weakly rounded at the beginning and neutral at the end.

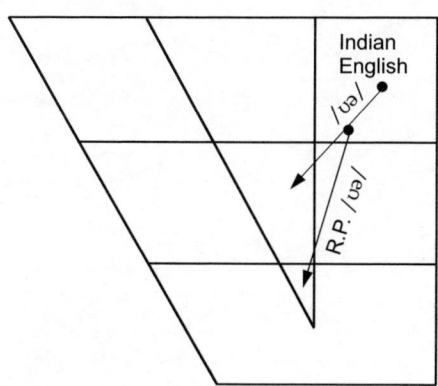

Fig. 21 / ʊə /

Spellings

- Stressed /ʊə/
  - *oo, ou, u + r*

	British R.P.	Indian English
poor	/pʊə/	[pʊər]
sure	/ʃʊə/	[ʃoːr]
tour	/tʊə/	[tuːr]

  Unstressed /ʊə/ has the prominence on the second element.

  Examples:

  | *influence* | /ˈinflʊəns/ | [ˈinflʊɛns] | |
  | *virtuous* | { /ˈvɜːtjʊəs/
 /ˈvɜːtʃʊəs/ | [ˈʊərtʃʊəs] | [ˈvərtʃʊəs] |

6. The Sounds of English: Consonants

6.1 There are twenty-four different consonants in English (British Received Pronunciation). These can be classified as shown in the chart on page 63.

Indian English differs from British R. P. in respect of the following:
- /t, d/ are sometimes retroflex /ṭ, ḍ/.
- /tʃ, dʒ, ʃ, ʒ/ are articulated with the tongue tip down.
- /v/ and /w/ are replaced by one phoneme
- /ʋ/ realized as a frictionless labio-dental /ʋ/ or weakly rounded /w/.
- /θ, ð/ are replaced by the plosives /t̪ʰ, d̪/.

6.2 Plosives

A *plosive* or *stop* consonant is produced by
- a complete closure of the air passage in the mouth;
- the holding of the *closure* and *compression* of the air coming from the lungs;
- a sudden *release* of air with *explosion*.

British R. P. has three pairs of plosive phonemes:
/p, b/ bilabial
/t, d/ alveolar (In Indian English these are often retroflex [ṭ, ḍ]).

/k, g/ velar

/p, t, k/ are voiceless and comparatively strong—called *fortis*; /b, d, g/ are voiced and comparatively weak—*lenis*.

In British R. P. /p, t, k,/ at the beginning of accented syllables are aspirated, that is, there is a strong puff of breath after the release of the plosive before the next vowel begins. The sound produced resembles फ in Hindi, though the puff of breath is not as strong as it is for फ. e.g.,

pack [pʰæk], *table* [ˈtʰeɪbl], *cage* [kʰeɪdʒ].

This aspiration is absent in Indian English, and lack of aspiration is a frequent cause of Indian English being unintelligible to native speakers.[1] It is desirable to have some aspiration in /p, t, k/ when they occur initially in accented syllables.

In R.P. the release of final plosives is sometimes almost inaudible.

When two stops come together, the first is not released; e.g., in act /ækt /, /k/ is held and only /t/ is released.

When a plosive is followed by a nasal consonant with the same place of articulation, the oral closure is retained and the compressed air is released through the nose by lowering the soft palate; e.g., in *button* (R.P. /ˈbʌtn/) /t/ is released through the nose.

When /t/ or /d/ is followed by /l/, the plosive is released laterally, that is, by retaining the alveolar contact in the middle and lowering the sides of the tongue. For example, /t/ in *bottle* (R.P. /ˈbɒtl/) has a lateral release.

6.2.1. Bilabial Plosives /p, b/

For /p, b/ the air passage in the mouth is closed by the two lips, and the soft palate is raised to shut off the nasal passage.

---

[1] Bansal, R.K. *The Intelligibility of Indian English*, Monograph No.4, Second (abridged) edition, The English and Foreign Languages University (earlier known as Central Institute of English and Foreign Languages), Hyderabad, 1976.

The Classification of English Consonants

Place → Manner ↓	Bilabial		Labio-dental		Dental		Alveolar		Post-alveolar	Palato-alveolar		Palatal		Velar		Glottal
	Voiceless	Voiced	v.l.	vd	v.l.	vd	v.l.	vd	vd	v.l.	vd	v.l.	vd	v.l.	vd	v.l.
Plosive	p	b					t	d						k	g	
Affricate										tʃ	dʒ					
Fricative			f	v	θ	ð	s	z		ʃ	ʒ					h
Nasal		m						n							ŋ	
Lateral								l								
Frictionless Continuant or Glide (Semi-vowel)		w							r				j		(w)	

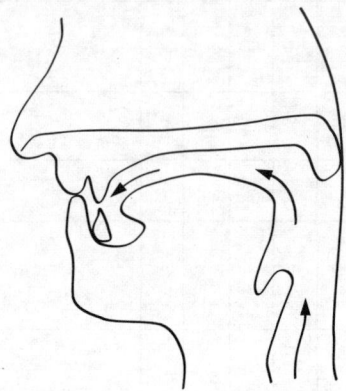

Fig. 22 /p, b/

The air from the lungs is compressed, and when the lips are separated, it is released with explosion. The vocal cords are held apart for /p/, but vibrate for /b/.

In British R.P. /p/ is aspirated at the beginning of accented syllables, as in *pair, pin, port, ap'point, pay, pray*. It is unaspirated after /s/ as in *spare, spin, sport*, and in unaccented positions as in *po'lite, pre'serve, 'upper*. /b/ is never aspirated in English.

Spellings

The sound /p/ is represented by the letter *p*. In *cupboard* (R.P. /ˈkʌbəd/) and *receipt* /rɪˈsiːt/, the letter *p* is silent.

The sound /b/ is represented by the letter *b*. In words like *comb, limb, thumb* and *debt, b* is silent.

In Indian English /p/ is unaspirated in all positions. It is necessary to aspirate it at the beginning of accented syllables when talking to native English speakers, because lack of aspiration in this position is likely to cause confusion between pairs like *pack* and *back*.

6.2.2 Dental Plosives in Indian English

Dental plosives /t̪ʰ/ and /d̪/ are used in Indian English instead of the fricatives /θ/ and /ð/ in words like *thank* and *then*. For international intelligibility it is necessary to use the fricative sounds.

6.2.3 Alveolar Plosives /t, d/

For /t, d/ the air passage in the mouth is closed by the tip of the tongue making a contact with the teeth-ridge and the rims of the tongue touching the upper side teeth. The soft palate is raised to shut off the nasal passage. The air from the lungs is compressed, and when the tip of the tongue is suddenly removed from the teeth-ridge, the air escapes with explosion. The vocal cords are held apart for /t/, but vibrate for /d/.

In British R.P. /t/ is aspirated at the beginning of accented syllables, as in *team, tone, top, at'tack, be'tween, train, tune*. The puff of breath for /t/ is weaker than it is for the sounds ठ and थ in Hindi. It is unaspirated after /s/, as in *steam, stone, stop*, and in unaccented positions, as in *'better, 'enter, 'liberty, to 'morrow*. /d/ is never aspirated in English.

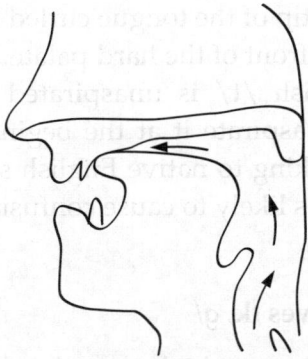

Fig. 23 /t, d/

In R P /t/ has a nasal release in words like *button, cotton, eaten* only if the vowel /ə/ between /t/ and /n/ is not pronounced. It is optional. It has a lateral release in words like *battle, little, settle*.

Spellings

/t/
- *t*
- *tt* as in settle.
- *ed* in past and past participate forms, after voiceless consonants other than /t /, e.g.,

talked	/tɔ:kt/
laughed	/lɑ:ft/
passed	/pɑ:st/

- /t/ *is silent in words* that have the spelling

  st + consonant letter *l* and mute *e*, e.g., ˈcastle, ˈwrestle, aˈpostle, eˈpistle, ˈjostle, ˈrustle and ˈChristmas and
  st + en, e.g. *fasten, hasten, chasten, listen, christen*.

/d/ *d, dd*

In Indian English /t/ and /d/ are often retroflex, that is, articulated by the tip of the tongue curled back and making a contact with the front of the hard palate.

In Indian English /t/ is unaspirated in all positions. It is necessary to aspirate it at the beginning of accented syllables when talking to native English speakers, because lack of aspiration is likely to cause confusion between pairs like *train* and *drain*.

6.2.4 Velar Plosives /k, g/

For /k, g/ the air passage in the mouth is closed completely by the back of the tongue making a contact with the soft

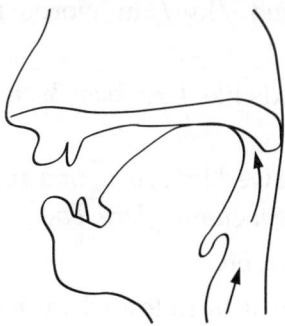

Fig. 24 /k, g/

palate. The nasal passage in also shut off by raising the soft palate. The air from the lungs is compressed, and when the tongue is suddenly removed from the soft palate, the air escapes with explosion. The vocal cords are wide apart for /k/, but vibrate for /g/.

In British R.P. /k/ is aspirated at the beginning of accented syllables, as in *cool, cold, corn, clean*. The puff of breath for /k/ is weaker than the puff of breath used to articulate the Hindi sound ख. /k/ is unaspirated after /s/, as in *school, scold, scorn,* and in unaccented positions, as in *ca'nal, col'lect, 'packing, 'equal*. /g/ is never aspirated in English.

Spellings

/k/
- *k*, e.g., *kind, basket, milk*.
- *c*, generally followed by *a, o, u,* or a consonant letter, also final *c*, e.g., *educate, call, come, cut, clean, music*.
- *cc + a, o, u*, e.g., *occasion, accord, occur*.
- *ck*, e.g., *attack, back, sick*.
- *qu*, e.g., *conquer, cheque*.
- *ch*, e.g., *character, stomach*.

- *qu* is pronounced /kw/ in words like *quality, queen, quiet*.
- *k* is silent in words like *knee, knife, know*.

/g/
- *g*, generally followed by *a, o, u*, or a consonant letter; also final, e.g., *gate, go, guard, glory, bag*.
- *g + e, i* in *get, give*, etc.
- *g* is silent when it is followed by *n* in the final/initial position in words e.g. *sign, gnome, reign, feign, design, foreign*.
- *gg* in *baggage*.

In Indian English /k/ is unaspirated in all positions. It is necessary to aspirate it at the beginning of accented syllables, when talking to native English speakers; otherwise there is a possibility of confusion between pairs like *cold* and *gold, cot* and *got*.

6.3 Affricates

Affricates are produced by a complete closure of the air passage and a slow release causing friction. The English palato-alveolar affricates /tʃ/ and /dʒ/ are treated as single phonemes and not sequences of two phonemes.

In the production of British R.P. /tʃ, dʒ/ the air passage in the mouth is completely closed by a contact between the tip and blade of the tongue and the teeth-ridge, the rims of the tongue making a contact with the upper side teeth. The front of the tongue is also raised towards the hard palate. The soft palate is raised to shut off the nasal passage.

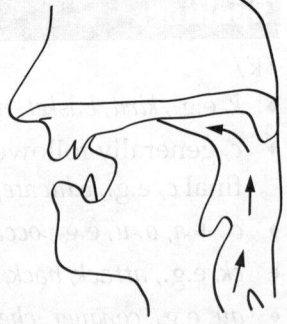

Fig. 25   /tʃ, dʒ/

When the air is released slowly, it escapes with friction between the front of the tongue and the hard palate and between the blade of the tongue and the teeth-ridge. The vocal cords are wide apart for /tʃ/ but vibrate for /dʒ/.

In British R.P. /tʃ, dʒ/ are always released even when followed by another plosive or affricate, as in

watch chain (tʃ + tʃ), *orange juice* (dʒ + dʒ).

In Indian English the first affricate is not released in such contexts.

Spellings

/tʃ/
- *ch*, e.g., *chair, such.*
- *tch*, e.g., *catch, watch.*
- *t + ure*, e.g., *furniture, nature, picture.*
- *t + ion* when preceded by *s*, e.g., *suggestion, question.*

/dʒ/
- *j* initial, e.g., *join, jump.*
- *g + e*, e.g., *general, gentle.*
- *dg*, e.g., *bridge, edge, judge.*
- *gg*, e.g., *suggest.*
- *di*, e.g., *soldier.*

Some Assamese speakers replace /tʃ/ by /s/.

6.4 Fricatives

Fricative consonants are produced by bringing two organs so near each other that the air stream has to pass through a narrow passage and comes out with audible friction. The following are the fricative phonemes in British R.P.

/f, v/   labio-dental
/θ, ð/   dental
/s, z/   alveolar
/ʃ, ʒ/   palato-alveolar
/h/   glottal

/f, θ, s, ʃ, h/ are fortis and voiceless; the others are lenis and voiced.

6.4.1 Labio-dental Fricatives—/ f /, British R.P. / v/

For /f, v/ the lower lip is brought very close to the edge of the upper teeth, making a light contact with it. The soft palate is raised to shut off the nasal passage. The air comes out between the lower lip and the upper teeth with friction. The vocal cords are wide apart for /f/, but vibrate for /v/.

Spellings

/f /
- f, e.g., *face*, *defend*, *leaf*.
- *ff*, medial and final, e.g., *afford*, *staff*.
- *ph*, e.g., *photograph*.

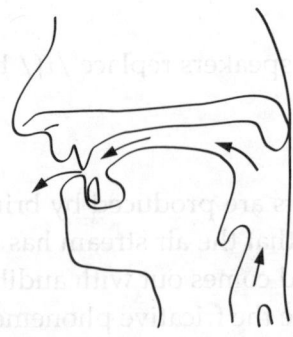

Fig. 26   /f/, R.P. /v/

- *gh*, e.g., *cough, rough*.
/v/
- *v*, e.g., *vain, cover, brave*.
- *f* in *of*.
- *ph* in *nephew*. (also pronounced /nefju:/)

Some Indian speakers replace /f/ by a bilabial plosive [pʰ]. It is necessary to distinguish between the two sounds in order to avoid confusion between pairs like the following:

/f/	[pʰ]
fair	pair
fall	pall
fear	pier
feel	peel
fine	pine
fool	pool
full	pull

There should be no complete closure for /f/, which is a labio-dental fricative.

Indian speakers use /f/ in place of /v/ in *of*, so that *of* and *off* are not distinguished. In other words they use a frictionless /ʊ/, which is so soft that it can hardly be heard at times. It is necessary to use a fricative /v/ when talking to native English speakers because the substitution of a weak /ʊ/ for /v/ is a very frequent cause of unintelligibility. /v/ can be produced easily by placing the upper teeth on the lower lip and pushing the air out, at the same time producing voice. /v/ is the voiced counterpart of /f/, the lower lip and the upper teeth being in the same position for both.

Some Bihari Hindi and Marathi speakers use [ʊʰ] for /v/.

Some Bengali speakers replace /v/ by /b/.

6.4.2 Dental Fricatives—British R.P. /θ, ð/

For R.P. /θ, ð/ the tip of the tongue is brought very near the edge of the upper teeth to make a light contact, and the soft palate is raised to shut off the nasal passage. The air passing between the tip and blade of the tongue and the upper teeth produces audible friction. The vocal cords are wide apart for /θ/ but vibrate for /ð/.

These two sounds are always spelt *th*.

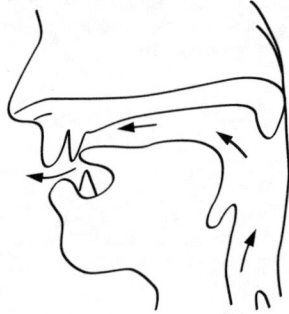

Fig. 27 R.P. /θ, ð/

Indian speakers generally use an aspirated dental plosive [t̪ʰ] in place of /θ/. Malayalam speakers use an unaspirated dental plosive [t̪].

It is necessary to use the dental fricative /θ/ when talking to native English speakers, because the substitution of a plosive can potentially lead to confusion between pairs like the following:

/θ/	/t/
fourth	fort
thank	tank
thin	tin
thinker	tinker
thought	taught

three   tree
through   true

A voiceless dental plosive [t̪] or [t̪ʰ] is often heard by a native English speaker as /t/.

/ð/ is always replaced in India by the dental plosive /d̪/. It is necessary to use the fricative /ð/ when talking to native English speakers in order to avoid confusion between pairs like the following:

/ð/   /d/
breathe   breed
there   dare
then   den
they   day
though   doe

A voiced dental plosive /d̪/ is likely to be heard by a native English speaker as /d/.

6.4.3 Alveolar Fricatives /s, z/

For /s, z/ the tip and the blade of the tongue are brought very near the teeth-ridge and the air comes out through a narrow groove along the middle of the tongue with

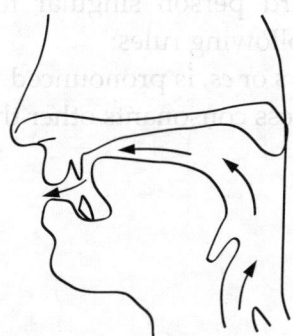

Fig. 28   /s, z/

audible friction. The soft palate is raised to shut off the nasal passage. The vocal cords are wide apart for /s/ but vibrate for /z/.

Spellings

/s/
- s, e.g., *single, slope, just, purpose, books.*
- ss, medial and final, e.g., *essence, confess, pass.*
- c, followed by *e, i*, e.g., *parcel, face, difference, city.*
- sc, initial and medial, e.g., *scene, science, obscene.*
- x, medial and final (pronounced /ks/), e.g., *box, explain.*

/z/
- s, medial and final, e.g., *poison, easy, compose, praise, bags.*
- ss, e.g., *scissors.*
- z, e.g., *zoo, zero.*
- zz, e.g., *puzzle.*
- x, medial (pronounced /gz/), e.g., *ex'act, ex'amine.*

The distribution of /s/ and /z/ in inflectional suffixes—in the plural and possessive forms of nouns and the present (simple) tense third person singular forms of verbs—is governed by the following rules:

The suffix, spelt *s* or *es*, is pronounced.
- /s/ after voiceless consonants other than /tʃ, s, ʃ/

  e.g.,
  caps
  cuts
  books
  takes
  laughs
  months

- /z/ after vowels and voiced consonants other than /dʒ, z, ʒ/, e.g.,

eyes	loves
hours	waves
replies	breathes
shows	children's
trees	forms
years	lines
robs	runs
heads	things
bags	hills

- /ɪz/ (/ɛz/ in Indian English) after /tʃ, dʒ, s, z, ʃ, ʒ/.

  e.g., catches
  judges
  influences
  passes
  noises
  washes
  barrages

In Indian English /z/ in inflectional suffixes is sometimes replaced by /s/. This leads to confusion between pairs like the following:

/z/	/s/
eyes	ice
falls	false
fears	fierce
his	hiss
knees	niece
peas	peace

Some Hindi speakers replace /z/ by /dʒ/.

6.4.4 Palato-alveolar Fricatives /ʃ, ʒ/

For British R.P. /ʃ, ʒ/ the tip and blade of the tongue are brought very near the teeth-ridge, and the front of the tongue is also raised towards the hard palate. The air passes through the narrow passage with audible friction. The soft palate is raised to shut off the nasal passage. The vocal cords are wide apart for /ʃ/, but vibrate for /ʒ/.

In Indian English /ʃ, ʒ/ are articulated with the tongue tip down and the front of the tongue brought near the post-alveolar region.

/ʒ/ does not occur initially.

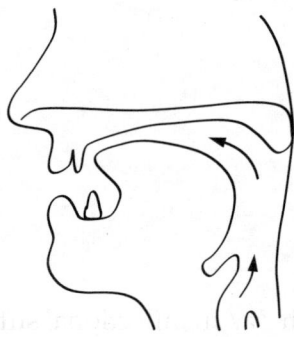

Fig. 29 R. P. /ʃ, ʒ/

Spellings

/ʃ/
- *sh*, e.g., *shade, shine, cushion, push.*
- *ch*, e.g., *machine.*
- *s + u*, e.g., *sure, sugar.*
- *-ti*, e.g., *nation, motion.*
- *-sci*, e.g., *conscience.*
- *-ci* e.g., *special, official.*
- *-ce*, e.g., *ocean.*

/ʒ/
- si, e.g., *decision, confusion.*
- s + u, e.g., *measure, pleasure.*
- *-ge* in French loan words e.g., *barrage.*

Some Assamese, Bihari Hindi and Oriya speakers replace /ʃ/ by /s/, with the result that there is confusion between the following pairs:

/ʃ/	/s/
shave	save
she	see
sheet	seat
shine	sign
shore	sore
short	sort

Many Indian speakers do not use /ʒ/ but replace it by /z/ or /dʒ/.

6.4.5 Glottal Fricative /h/

/h/ is produced by the air coming through a narrow glottis with audible friction; the sound can also be regarded as a voiceless beginning of the following vowel. It does not occur finally. *h* is silent after *g* word initially, e.g., *ghost, ghastly.*

6.5 Nasals

For the production of nasal consonants a complete closure is made in the mouth, but the soft palate is lowered and the air comes out through the nose.

There are three nasal phonemes in English.

| /m/ | bilabial |
| /n/ | alveolar |

/ŋ/   velar

Nasals are in some ways vowel-like; they are frictionless continuants and can sometimes be syllabic, e.g., /n/ in *button* (R.P. /ˈbʌtn/), *frighten* (R.P. /ˈfraɪtn/).

6.5.1 Bilabial Nasal /m/

For /m/ the mouth passage is completely closed by the lips. The soft palate is lowered and the air comes out through the nose. The vocal cords are in vibration.

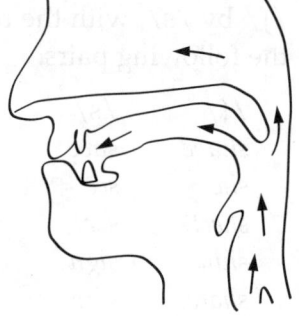

Fig. 30   /m/

Spellings

- *m*, e.g., *mad, among, come*.
- *mm*, medial, e.g., *summer, hammer*.
- *mb*, final, e.g., *limb, thumb*.
- *mn*, final, e.g., *autumn*.

6.5.2 Alveolar Nasal /n/

For /n/ the tip of the tongue makes a closure against the teeth-ridge and the rims of the tongue are against the upper side teeth. The soft palate is lowered and the air comes out through the nose. The vocal cords vibrate.

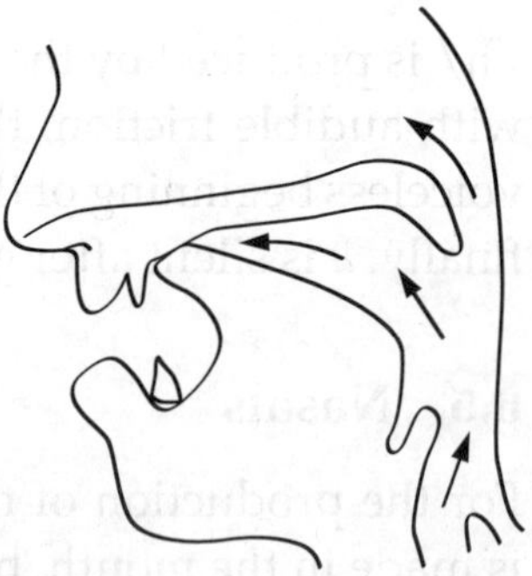

/n/ can be syllabic in British R.P. as in *cotton* /ˈkɒtn/, *button* /ˈbʌtn/, *sudden* /ˈsʌdn/, *listen* /ˈlɪsn/. It is dental before /θ, ð/ as in *tenth* /tenθ/.

Fig. 31   /n/

Spellings

- *n*, e.g., *no, opinion, run.*
- *nn*, medial, e.g., *manner, running.*
- *kn*, initial, e.g., *known, knife.*
- *gn*, inital and final e.g., *gnome, sign.*
- *mn*, initial, e.g., *mnemonic.*
- *pn*, initial, e.g., *pneumatic, pneumonia.*

6.5.3 Velar Nasal /ŋ/

For /ŋ/ the back of the tongue makes a closure with the soft palate, which is lowered so that the air escapes through the nose. The vocal cords vibrate.

/ŋ/ does not occur initially.

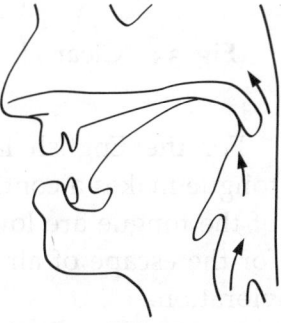

Fig. 32 /ŋ/

Spellings

- *ng*, e.g., *sing, singer, song, long, hang.*
- *n* + /k/, e.g., *think, monkey, uncle.*

In British R.P. final *ng* is pronounced /ŋ/, e.g., *sing* /sɪŋ/; in derivatives from verbs ending in /ŋ/, no /g/ is added after /ŋ/, e.g., *singer* /ˈsɪŋə/. In other words medial *ng* is pronounced /ŋg/, as in *finger* /ˈfɪŋgə/, *longer* /ˈlɔŋgə/.

Some Indian speakers add /g/ after /ŋ/ in words like *singer, things, writings.*

6.6 Lateral /l/

For a lateral consonant there is a closure in the middle and the air comes out through the sides.

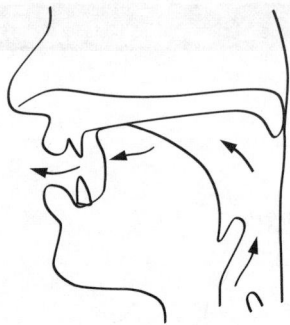
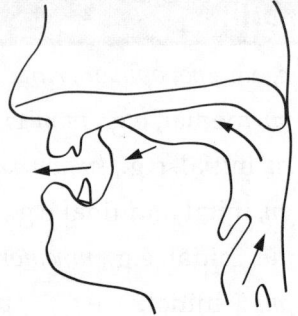

Fig. 33   Clear /l/   Fig. 34   Dark /ʃ/

For the English lateral phoneme /l/, the tip of the tongue makes a contact with the teeth-ridge but the sides of the tongue are lowered so that there is a free passage for the escape of air on the sides. The vocal cords are in vibration.

In British R.P. two varieties of /l/ are used; a clear variety /l/, for which the front of the tongue is also raised towards the hard palate, is used before vowels and /j/. A dark variety [ɫ], for which the back of the tongue is raised towards the soft palate, is used in other positions. Indian English has only the clear variety.

/l/ is dental before /θ, ð/ as in *health*.

In R.P. /l/ is syllabic in words like *bottle* /ˈbɒtl/ and *cattle* /ˈkætl/.

Spellings

- *l*, e.g., *laugh, glad, oil*.
- *ll*, e.g., *yellow, kill*.
- /l/ is silent in words like *walk, should, half, calm*.

6.7 Post-alveolar Frictionless Continuant /r/

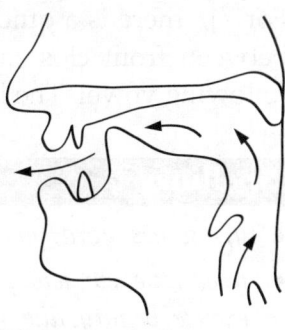

Fig. 35 /r/

The commonest variety of R.P. /r/ is produced by raising the tip of the tongue towards the back of the teeth-ridge—a slight retroflexion, so to say. The air comes out through the mouth without any friction. The soft palate is raised to shut off the nasal passage.

Even though the sound is vowel-like, it is treated as a consonant because it takes the position associated with consonants, e.g., *bat, cat, rat*.

In R.P. /r/ is used only before vowels; it does not occur finally and before consonants.

e.g., better /ˈbetə/
burst /bɜːst/

here /hɪə/ (but when the next word begins with a vowel, a linking /r/ is inserted, e.g., *Here it is*. /hɪər ɪt ɪz/.

A voiced fricative /r/ is used after /d/ as in *dry, draw*. A voiceless fricative /r/ is used after accented /p, t, k/ as in *pray, try, cream*. An alveolar flap is also used between two vowels as in *very* and after /θ/ as in *three*.

In Indian English /r/ is often retained in all positions. Some speakers use the flapped variety in most positions.

6.8 Semi-Vowels

A semi-vowel is a vowel glide to a more prominent sound in the same syllable. English /j/ is a glide from /iː/ and /w/ is a glide from /uː/. Semi-vowels are treated as consonants because they take the positions normally associated with consonants, e.g., *pet, get, set, yet, wet*.

6.8.1 Unrounded Palatal Semi-Vowel /j/

For /j/ there is a quick tongue movement from a position between front close and half-close to the position of the following vowel. The lips are neutral or spread.

Spellings

- *y*, e.g., *yes, yard, young, beyond*.
- *u, eau, ue, ew, iew*, pronounced, /ju:/, e.g., *union, pupil, tube, excuse, beauty, due, new, view, human*.

6.8.2 Labio-velar semi-vowel /w/

For /w/ the tongue moves quickly from a position between back close and half-close to the position for the following vowel. The lips are rounded.

Spellings

- *w*, e.g., *way, well, west*
- *wh*, e.g., *when, which, where*.
- *q, g, + u*, e.g., *quick, queen, quality, language*.

In Indian English, /w/ is generally replaced by /ʊ/. Even when [w] occurs, it is a free variant of /ʊ/. It is necessary to acquire both /w/ and /v/ and make a distinction between pairs like the following:

/w/	/v/
while	vile
west	vest
why	vie

The substitution of /ʊ/ for /w/ is one of the most frequent causes of Indian English being unintelligible to native English speakers. /w/ can be acquired easily by rounding the lips as we would for /u:/, filling the mouth with the air we are to breathe out and then breathing out by quickly moving to the vowel that follows /w/ in a word.

6.9 Consonant Clusters

Two or more consonants sometimes come together at the beginning or the end of an English syllable. Here is a list of common English consonant clusters.

6.9.1 Initial Clusters (2 or 3 consonants)

- /p/ as first member
  - /pl-/   play, please, plenty
  - /pr-/   pray, press, price
  - /pj-/   pupil, pure
- /b/ as first member
  - /bl-/   black, blood, blue
  - /br-/   brave, bring, brush
  - /bj-/   beauty
- /t/ as first member
  - /tr-/   train, treasure, true
  - /tj-/   tube, tune, Tuesday
  - /tw-/   twist, twelve, twice
- /d/ as first member
  - /dr-   draw, dream, drop
  - /dj-/   due, during, duty
  - /dw-/   dwell
- /k/ as first member
  - /kl-/   class, clean, cloth
  - /kr-/   cry, crush, crowd
  - /kj-/   cure, curious
  - /kw-/   quality, queen, quick
- /g/ as first member
  - /gl-/   glad, glass, glory
  - /gr-/   grass, great, green
- /f/ as first member
  - /fl/   flag, float , fly
  - /fr-/   free, fresh, from
  - /fj-/   few, funeral, future
- /v/ as first member
  - /vj-/   view

- /θ/ as first member
  - /θr-/ three, through, throw
  - /θw-/ thwart
- /s/ as first member
  - 2 consonants
    - /sp-/ speak, special, spend
    - /st-/ stamp, stay, sticks
    - /sk-/ school, scarce, scold
    - /sf-/ sphere
    - /sm-/ small, smoke, smooth
    - /sn-/ snow, snake
    - /sl-/ sleep, slope, slow
    - /sj/ suit, sewer (also /suːt/, /ˈsuːəʳ/)
    - /sw-/ swear, sweet, swim
  - 3 consonants
    - /spl-/ split, splendid
    - /spr-/ spread, spring
    - /spj-/ spurious
    - /str-/ straight, stream, strike
    - /stj-/ stupid, student
    - /skr-/ screen, screw, scratch
    - /skw-/ square
- /h/ as first member
  - /hj-/ human
- /m/ as first member
  - /mj-/ music
- /n/ as first member
  - /nj-/ new, nuisance

Some Hindi and Urdu speakers have difficulty with initial consonant clusters with /s/. They insert a vowel, /ə/ or /ɪ/, before /sp-/, /st-/, /sk-/, /sm-/, /str-/, in words like *speech, start, state, stay, still, study, school, small, street* and *strength*. To get over this difficulty one should prolong /s/ and then add the following consonant. The length of /s/ should be gradually reduced.

6.9.2 Final Clusters (2, 3 or 4 consonants)

- /p/ as final element
  - /-mp/ — *camp, damp, jump*
  - /-lp/ — *help*
- /t/ as final element
  - 2 consonants
    - /-pt/ — *adopt, except, interrupt*
    - /-kt/ — *act, collect, district*
    - /-tʃt/ — *reached, searched*
    - /-ft/ — *laughed, soft*
    - /-st/ — *almost, beast, chest*
    - /-ʃt/ — *pushed, rushed, washed*
    - /-nt/ — *absent, content*
    - /-lt/ — *belt, difficult, fault*
  - 3 consonants
    - /-dst/ — *midst*
    - /-kst/ — *fixed, mixed, next*
    - /-skt/ — *asked*
    - /-mpt/ — *attempt, prompt, tempt*
    - /-ntʃt/ — *lunched*
    - /-nst/ — *advanced, against, danced*
    - /-ŋkt/ — *thanked*
    - /ŋst/ — *amongst*
    - /-lpt/ — *helped*
    - /-lkt/ — *milked*
    - /-lst/ — *whilst*
- /b/ as final element
  - /-lb/ — *bulb*
- /d/ as final element
  - /-bd/ — *robbed, rubbed*
  - /-gd/ — *begged*
  - /-dʒd/ — *judged*
  - /-vd/ — *loved, proved, saved*
  - /-ðd/ — *breathed*
  - /-zd/ — *confused, raised, surprised*

	/-md/	ashamed
	/-nd/	band, command, depend
	/-ŋd/	hanged
	/-ld/	bold, child, field, fold, gold
♦ /k/ as final element	/-sk/	ask, desk
	/-ŋk/	bank, drink, pink,
	/-lk/	milk, silk
♦ /tʃ/ as final element	/-ntʃ/	branch, lunch, pinch
♦ /dʒ/ as final element	/-ndʒ/	arrange, change, orange
♦ /f/ as final element	/-lf/	self
	/-mf/	triumph
♦ /v/ as final element	/-lv/	solve
♦ /θ/ as final element		
2 consonants	/-pθ/	depth
	/tθ/	eighth
	/dθ/	breadth
	/fθ/	fifth
	/-mθ/	warmth
	/-nθ/	month, ninth, tenth
	/-ŋθ/	length, strength
	/-lθ/	health, wealth
3 consonants	/-ksθ/	sixth
	/-lfθ/	twelfth
♦ /s/ as final element		
2 consonants	/-ps/	caps, hopes, maps
	/-ts/	eats, hates, roots
	/-ks/	axe, box, fix, socks, sticks
	/-fs/	laughs, proofs

The Sounds of English—Consonants

	/-θs/	fourths
	/-ns/	absence, balance, dance
	/-ls/	else, false
3 consonants	/-pts/	adopts
	/-pθs/	depths
	/-tθs/	eighths
	/-kts/	acts, directs, elects
	/-fts/	lifts
	/-sps/	wasps
	/-sts/	beasts, requests, tests
	/-sks/	asks, desks
	/-mps/	lamps, stamps
	/-mfs/	triumphs
	/-nts/	aunts, parents, tents
	/-nθs/	months, tenths
	/-ŋks/	banks, thanks, thinks
	/-lps/	helps
	/-lts/	belts, faults, melts
	/-lks/	silks
4 consonants	/-ksθts/	texts
	/-ksθs/	sixths
	/-mpts/	tempts
	/-lfθs/	twelfths

♦ /z/ as final element

2 consonants	/-bz/	clubs, robs
	/-dz/	heads, leads, outwards
	/-gz/	bags, dogs, eggs
	/-vz/	lives, knives, saves
	/-ðz/	breathes
	/-mz/	names, steams, times
	/-nz/	beans, fans, inns
	/-ŋz/	hangs, rings, stockings, things
	/-lz/	balls, mills, sells

3 consonants	/-ndz/	*hands, islands, sends*
	/-lbz/	*bulbs*
	/-ldz/	*builds, folds, holds*
	/lvz/	*solves*
	/-lmz/	*films*
♦ /m/ as final element	/-lm/	*film*

7. Word Stress

7.1 Word Stress

Word stress is an important feature of English. In words of more than one syllable, not all the syllables are equally prominent. Those that are more prominent than others are said to receive the stress. Most modern dictionaries generally indicate the location of word stress by putting a vertical line above/below and in front of the stressed syllable; and because there are very few rules in the matter, it is necessary to refer to the dictionary to find out the stress pattern.

The relative prominence of a syllable may be due to stress, that is, greater breath force, greater muscular effort, and greater amplitude of vibration of the vocal cords in the case of voiced sounds. Very often stress and pitch change work together to make a syllable prominent. The quality of the sounds and their length also contribute to prominence.

The syllable on which there is a pitch change is said to have the *primary* or *tonic* stress. Any other prominent syllable is said to have *secondary* stress. Primary stress is marked with a vertical bar above and in front of the syllable to which it refers, secondary stress with a bar below and in front of the syllable.

Examples

2 syllables

Stress on the first syllable

ˈable, ˈbaggage, ˈcaptain, ˈdamage, ˈeager, ˈkidney, ˈdentist, ˈmaster, ˈpackage, ˈtackle.

Stress on the second syllable:

aˈbout, beˈcause, caˈnal, deˈceive, efˈfect, enˈrol, posˈsess, deˈlight, beˈside, reˈcourse.

3 syllables

Primary stress on the first syllable

ˈaccident, ˈbicycle, ˈcalcuˌlate, ˈdelicate, ˈeduˌcate, ˈrecogˌnise, ˈrectiˌfy, ˈpermeˌate, ˈforeigner, ˈquarrelsome.

Primary stress on the second syllable

acˈcustom, comˈmittee, deˈliver, eˈlastic, hoˈrizon, pyˈjama, reˈactor, faˈmiliar, sulˈphuric, desˈcribing.

Primary stress on the third syllable

ˌdisapˈpoint, ˌenterˈtain, ˌrecomˈmend, ˌunderˈstand, ˌsuperˈsede, ˌmillioˈnaire, ˌinhuˈmane, ˌdecomˈpose.

7.2 Stress Shift

It should not be assumed that words with the same stem will keep the primary stress on the same syllable.
  Indeed, stress shift in derivatives is quite normal, e.g.,

aˈcademy, ˌacaˈdemic, aˌcadeˈmician
bacˈteria, bacˌteriˈology, bacˌterioˈlogical
ˌindiˈvidual, ˌindiˌviduˈality, ˌindiˌviduaˈlistic
ˈpolitics, poˈlitical, ˌpoliˈtician.

7.3 Historical Reasons for Shift

The reasons for complexity in word stress in English lie in history. The language is drawn from two main sources, Germanic and Romance. In the first, words normally had stress at the beginning; in the second, on the contrary, the last syllable was usually the most prominent, and it is the interaction of these two principles that has produced the stress patterns of modern English.

7.4 Compound Words

In compound words, that is, words consisting of combinations of two words, the primary stress is generally on one element—usually the first.

Examples

2 elements
Primary stress on the first element

ˈanything
ˈbackbone
ˈearthquake
ˈgoldsmith

Sometimes both elements are stressed, but the tonic stress is on the second element. This is shown by an oblique bar pointing downwards to indicate the tonic stress and a vertical bar to indicate the pre-tonic stress.

ˈafterˈnoon
ˈhalf-ˈhour
ˈlong-ˈlived
ˈmiddle-ˈaged
ˈnorth-ˈwest

In connected speech one of the two stresses is dropped to suit the rhythm of the sentence. For example, in the sentence,

She enjoys her ˈafternoon ˈtea.

the stress on *noon* is dropped because of the following word *tea* which being the last content word in the information focus, is the tonic syllable.

Similarly in the sentence,

Most of the ˈmiddle-aged ˈwomen in the loˈcality ˈturned up for the ˈcamp.

the stress on *aged* is dropped because of the stress on the first syllable of *women* which is adjacent to *aged*.

3 elements

Primary (tonic) stress on the second element

ˈhot-ˈwater-ˌbottle
ˈwaste-ˈpaper-ˌbasket

7.5 Stress Change According to Function

There are a number of words of two syllables in which the accentual pattern depends on whether the word is used as a noun, an adjective, or a verb. The accent is on the first syllable when the word is a noun or an adjective and on the second syllable when it is a verb

Examples			
ˈobject (n.)	/ˈɒbdʒɪkt/	obˈject (v.)	/əbˈdʒekt/
ˈperfect (adj.)	/ˈpɜːfɪkt/	perˈfect (v.)	/pəˈfekt/
ˈproduce (n.)	/ˈprɒdjuːs/	proˈduce (v.)	/prəˈdjuːs/
ˈprogress (n.)	/ˈprəʊgres/	proˈgress (v.)	/prəʊˈgres/
ˈrecord (n.)	/ˈrekɔːd/	reˈcord (v.)	/rɪˈkɔːd/
ˈimport (n.)	/ˈɪmpɔːt/	imˈport (v.)	/ɪmˈpɔːt/
ˈsubject (n.)	/ˈsʌbdʒɪkt/	subˈject (v.)	/səbˈdʒekt/
ˈincrease (n.)	/ˈɪnkriːs/	inˈcrease (v.)	/ɪnˈkriːs/

7.6 Word Stress in Indian English

The patterns of word stress in English are not well organised. In some cases, a pattern different from that in British R.P. is used.

For example, the feature of change in stress according to the function of the word is not always found in Indian English. *Absent* is generally stressed on the first syllable, both as an adjective and as a verb. *Object* is stressed on the first syllable, both as a noun and a verb.

Here are some other examples of word stress patterns in Indian English that diverge from R.P.

conduct (v.), develop, activity, already, correct, expect, hotel, industrial, mistake, occur and *prefer* are stressed on the first syllable by some speakers instead of the second.

atmosphere, industry, minister, record (n.), refuge, written and *yesterday* are stressed on the second syllable by some speakers instead of the first.

It is necessary to use the correct pattern of word stress when talking to native English speakers, because wrong word stress, that is, one different from that used in native English, is the most frequent cause of the unintelligibility of Indian English.[1]

7.7 Rules for Stress Patterns

Here are a few rules for stress patterns in English words:
- All English words have some stress, primary or secondary, on the first or the second syllable.
- Words with weak prefixes are stressed on the root, and not the prefix, e.g., a'broad, a'cross, ad'mit, ad'vice, a'head,

---
[1] R.K. Bansal, The Intelligibility of Indian English, Monograph No. 4, The English and Foreign Languages University, (earlier known as Central Institute of English and Foreign Languages), Hyderabad, Second (abridged) edition, 1976.

a'lone, a'loud, a'mount, a'part, at'tend, be'low, be'tween, com'pose, cor'rect, de'velop, ex'pect, oc'cur, pre'fer, re'duce.

♦ The inflectional suffixes *-es*, *-ing*, *-ed*, and the following derivational suffixes do not affect the stress: *-age, -dom, -en, -er, -ess, -ful, -fy, -less, -let, -ly, -ment, -ness, -or, -some, -ward*.

Examples

match	'matches
be'gin	be'ginning
want	'wanted
break	'breakage
free	'freedom
bright	'brighten
board	'boarder
god	'goddess
care	'careful
class	'classify
aim	'aimless
book	'booklet
bad	'badly
ap'point	ap'pointment
'bitter	'bitterness
'conquer	'conqueror
fear	'fearsome
back	'backward

♦ Words ending in *-ion* have the primary stress on the last syllable but one, e.g., ˌappli'cation, ˌcivili'zation, ˌcompo'sition, ˌconver'sation, ˌculti'vation, deˌtermi'nation, exˌami'nation, iˌmagi'nation, ˌintro'duction, ˌqualifi'cation.

♦ Words ending in *-ic, -ical, -cally*, have the primary stress on the syllable preceding the suffix, e.g., aˌpolo'getic,

eˈlectric, eˈlectrical, gramˈmatical, ˌpatriˈotic, poˈlitical, poˈ-
litically, ˌscienˈtific, ˌsympaˈthetic, ˌsympaˈthetically.

- Words ending in *-ity*, are stressed on the syllable preceding the suffix, that is, on the third syllable from the end—the ante-penultimate syllable, e.g., acˈtivity, ˌcuriˈosity, ˌelecˈtricity, eˈquality, ˌgeneˈrosity, moˈrality, neˈcessity, oˌrigiˈnatity, ˌpossiˈbility, ˌprobaˈbility.

- Words ending in *-ial*, *-ially* have the primary stress on the syllable preceding the suffix, e.g., ˌartiˈficial ˌcereˈmonial, ˌconfiˈdential, ˌconfiˈdentially, esˈsential, esˈsentially, inˈdustrial, meˈmorial, ofˈficial, ˌpresiˈdential.

- In words of more than two syllables ending in *-ate*, the primary stress is placed two syllables before the suffix, that is, on the third syllable from the end, e.g., ˈcompliˌcate, ˈcultiˌvate, ˈeduˌcate, ˈfortunate, ˈseparate (adj.), ˈsepaˌrate (v.)

- Words ending in *-ian* are stressed on the syllable preceding the suffix, e.g., ˌelecˈtrician, liˈbrarian, muˈsician, ˌpoliˈtician.

- Words ending in *-ious* are stressed on the syllable preceding the suffix, e.g., ˈanxious, inˈdustrious, inˈjurious, laˈborious, luˈxurious, reˈbellious, vicˈtorious.

- The following suffixes take the primary stress on their first syllable:

-aire	ˌmillioˈnaire
-eer	caˈreer
-ental	ˌfundaˈmental
-ential	ˌexisˈtential
-esce	ˌacquiˈesce
-escence	ˌefferˈvescence
-esque	groˈtesque
-ique	phyˈsique
-itis	neuˈritis

8. Features of Connected Speech

8.1 Stress in Connected Speech : Rhythm

In the chapter on word stress we saw that words in isolation had varying stress patterns. Of the several syllables in each word only one or two syllables were stressed or strong while the others were unstressed or weak. So each word had a combination of stressed and unstressed syllables.

Similarly, when words combine to form sentences not all of them are stressed. For example, in the sentence, *She* ˈ*went to the* ˈ*cinema* only the words *went* and the first syllable of ˈ*cinema* are stressed. The words *she, to, the* and the last two syllables of ˈ*cinema* i.e. *ne* and *ma* are unstressed. It is on this alternation of stressed and unstressed syllables that the rhythm of English depends. It would, therefore, sound odd if we were to stress every word in an English sentence.

 Look at the following sentences and listen to them.

ˈGive[1] them the ˈpearls.
He ˈparked his ˈcar in the ˈyard.
ˈDon't let him ˈtake it from you.
Shall we ˈmeet them toˈmorrow?
Inˈvite them to the ˈmeeting.
ˈSeveral of them have ˈleft.
It ˈstarted to ˈrain ˈheavily in the ˈevening.

---

[1] In connected speech the stress mark (ˈ) (in the written representation) is used on single-syllable words also as in ˈ*give* and ˈ*pearls*.

Notice that the first three sentences have only single-syllable words and not all of them are stressed. The next three sentences have both single-syllable words and words of more than one syllable. The speaker says all the sentences moving quickly from one stressed syllable to the next, gliding over the unstressed syllables between them (particularly when there are many of them) and weakening them. This is done to maintain the more or less regular beat provided by the stressed syllables. Also, notice that the syllables of words of more than one syllable which receive primary stress when the word is said in isolation are potentially those that will receive the stress when the word occurs in a sentence. Thus the words to'morrow, in'vite, 'meeting, 'several receive stress on the same syllable in sentences as they would if they were said in isolation.

As has already been said, the rhythm of a sentence depends on the number of stressed syllables and weak or unstressed syllables between them. In the first sentence the words *give* and *pearls* are stressed and there are two unstressed syllables —*them* and *the* between them. In the second sentence there are three stressed syllables—*parked*, *car*, *yard*. There is one weak syllable—*his* between *parked* and *car* and two weak syllables—*in, the* between *car* and *yard*. In the fifth sentence there are three weak syllables between the stressed syllables —'vite and 'meet—them, to, the.

In the sixth sentence there are four weak syllables—ral, of, them, have between 'sev and 'left. In the last sentence there are two weak syllables between 'start and 'rain—ed and to, no weak syllable between 'rain and 'heav and four weak syllables between 'heav and 'even—i, ly, in the.

From the sentences it is evident that the number of unstressed syllables between stressed syllables can vary from nil to four sometimes even within the same sentence. Consequently, the rhythm of English sentences varies depending on the number of stressed syllables they have and the number of unstressed syllables between them, that is, the fewer the unstressed between stressed syllables, the slower and heavier the rhythm, and the larger the number of unstressed syllables, the faster and lighter the rhythm.

This brings us to the kinds of words that are normally stressed in utterances. Certain words, by the very nature of their function in that they are likely to be more important in conveying the meaning of the whole utterance, are more likely than others to receive stress. These are nouns, main verbs, adjectives, adverbs, demonstrative and interrogative pronouns, and the negative *not*. Look at the sentences above for the kinds of words that are normally stressed. Words that are not important for meaning i.e. structure words, are generally unstressed.

There are, however, exceptions to this rule. There are contexts in which content words are <u>not</u> stressed and those in which structure words <u>are</u> stressed.

Look at the following sentences in which some content words are not stressed.

 If your ʹhands and ʹfeet are ʹwarm your ʹwhole ʹbody will be warm.
She ʹhasn't got the ʹglasses we're ʹlooking for.
He has the ʹlatest eʹdition of this ʹbook.

In the first sentence, notice that the content word *warm* is not stressed when it occurs the second time, because it gives no new information. In addition, such omission of stress on the repeated word *warm* helps to focus the listener's attention on the importance of the preceding content word *body* which gives the listener new information.

In the second sentence, the word *got* is not stressed, even though it is a content word, in order to emphasise the word *hasn't* which precedes it and *glasses* which follows it.

In the third sentence, though *has* is the main verb it is not stressed because *have* is not stressed when it means 'to possess'.

Sometimes a structure word may be stressed owing to its meaning and position in a sentence. Compare the following sentences, for example.

There 'aren't enough 'clothes to 'choose from.
There's e'nough 'room for us 'all.
Have you 'got enough 'room?

In the first sentence, the determiner *enough* is unstressed because the negation in *aren't* takes precedence over it. In the second sentence, *enough* is stressed because it adds to the meaning of the word *room*. In the third sentence *enough* is not stressed because the main verb *got* is related to *room*. In other words, the focus is on the availability of space. Stress at the level of the sentence is therefore much freer than at the level of the word.

Structure words in English may be stressed when they occur in the final position in utterances, or are used for emphasis or contrast. Look at the following examples.

- A : D'you 'think you can 'handle it on your 'own?
  B : Of 'course I 'can.

- A : 'Is that 'your 'bicycle?
  B : 'No. That's 'his.

- A : We've 'waited for 'two 'hours! I 'don't think 'C's 'coming.
  B : But he 'said he 'is coming.

- A : D'you 'want a 'pen or a 'pencil?
  B : I 'want a 'pen' and a 'pencil.

- A : Would you 'like to 'rest for a 'while.
  B : 'Yes. I 'would.

In the first dialogue, the auxiliary verb *can* is stressed because the speaker wishes to emphasise the fact that he *can* handle a situation/problem on his own.

In the second dialogue, the possessives *your* and *his* are stressed to bring out the contrast between *your* bicycle and *his*.

In the third dialogue, *is* receives stress for emphasis.

In the fourth dialogue *and* is stressed in contrast to *or*.

In the last dialogue, the auxiliary *would* is stressed. This generally happens when an auxiliary occurs in the final position in an utterance.

Words that are normally stressed in native English are sometimes left unstressed in Indian English. This is one reason why Indian English is sometimes unintelligible to native English speakers. This feature is particularly noticeable in noun phrases, where either the headword or one of the modifiers is sometimes left unstressed by Indian speakers.

Examples:

- ˈseveral other ˈthings — *other* not stressed; close juncture between *several* and *other*.
- ˈchemical engineering — *engineering* not stressed
- ˈIndian Students' ˈHostel — *Students'* not stressed.
- ˈurban centres — *centres* not stressed.
- ˈeighty-nine — *nine* not stressed.
- a ˈgreat need of — *need* not stressed.
- Biˈhar State ˈTransport — *State* not stressed.
- ˈEast Godavari ˈDistrict — *Godavari* not accented; close juncture between *East* and *Godavari*

- ˈCentral Institute of ˈEnglish — *Institute* not stressed.
- ˈArts College — *College* not stressed.

8.2 Weak Forms

Another important feature of English stress patterns is that unstressed syllables *between* the stressed syllables tend to become reduced. This phenomenon has become steadily more marked as the language has developed. The speaking voice seems almost to *take aim* at each successive strong syllable, and to glide over the intervening weak syllables. The reduction is most marked in quick and informal speech. For the learner of the language as well as for the student of phonetics, alterations in vowel quality as between the strong and the weak forms of the same word must be noted.

Examples:

	Weak form in British R.P.		Example
Articles			
a	/ə/		/əˈbuk/
an	/ən/		/ənˈeg/
the	/ðɪ/	before a vowel	/ðɪˈɑːmɪ/
	/ðə/	before a consonant	/ðəˈteibl/
Pronouns			
he	/hɪ/		/hɪ went həum/
she	/ʃɪ/		/ʃɪ left ɜːlɪ/
you	/jʊ/		/jʊ kən miːt hɪm təˈmɒrəu/
we	/wɪ/		/wɪə leit/

	Weak form in British R.P.	Example
her	/hə/	/wɒts hə neɪm/
me	/mɪ/	/gɪv mɪ sʌm/
them	/ðəm/	/liːv ðəm əˈləʊn/
us	/əs/	/liːvəs əˈləʊn/
Verbs		
am	/əm, m/	/əɪmˈkʌmɪŋ/
are	/ə/	/wɪəˈkʌmɪŋ/
can	/kən/	/juːkənˈgəʊ/
does (aux.)	/dəz/	/ˈwɒt dəzhiːˈwant/
had (aux.)	/həd, əd, d/	/wiːdˈfɪnɪʃt/
has (aux.)	/həz, əz, z, s/	/hiːzˈleft/, /ɪtsˈgɒn/
have (aux.)	I həv.əv, v /	/aivˈtəʊldjuː/
is	/z,s/	/hiːzˈhɪə/
shall	/ʃ/	/ˈwɒtʃl wiː ˈduː/
was	/wəz/	/hiːwəz ˈpreznt/
were	/ wə/	/juːwə ˈleɪt /
will	/l/	/ail ˈhelp juː/
would	/əd, d/	/aid ˈraðə ˈsteɪ in bed/
Conjunctions		
and	/ənd, an, n/	/ˈʌp ən ˈdaʊn/
as	/əz/	/trai əz ˈhɑːd əz juːˈkæn/
than	/ðən/	/hiːz ˈtɔːlə ðən miː/
that	/ðət/	/hiːtəʊld miː ðət hiː wəz ˈkʌmɪŋ/

Prepositions[2]

at	/ət/		/ˈlʊk ət ðə ˈblækbɔːd/
for	/fə/		/ðɪs ɪz fə ˈjuː/
from	/frəm/		/hiːˈkʌmz frəm ˈdeli/
of	/əv/		/ə ˈkʌpəvˈtiː/
to	/tə/	before a consonant	/aɪm ˈɡəʊɪŋ tə ˈdeli/
	/tu/	before a vowel	/aɪm ˈɡəʊɪŋ tu ˈɑːsk hɪm əbaʊt ɪt/

Weak forms are not always used in Indian English. Sometimes the weak form used is different from that in British R.P. The common Indian pronunciations of some of the words listed above are as follows:

a [e], *an* [ɛn], *the* [d̪ə] even before vowels.
are [ar], *can* [kæn], *had* [hæd], *is* [ɪz], *shall* [ʃæl]
and [ænd], *as* [æz], *that* [d̪æt], *at* [æt]
for [fɒr], *from* [frɒm], *of* [ɒf], *to* [tu] in all positions.

Practice in Weak Forms
Here is a list of phrases and sentences for pronunciation practice. Each contains one or more weak forms, and, naturally, one or more stressed syllables.

Ten rupees *a* kilo. /ə/
I want *an* old one. /ən/
The old men. /ðɪ/
I*'m* not coming. /m/
Mohan*'s* not staying here. /z/
They*'re* all stupid. /ər/

---

[2] Of the prepositions in English only the prepositions given above have weak forms.

He *was* brilliant even *as a* boy. /wəz/, /əz/, /ə/
They *were* eating. /wər/
I*'ve* never met *him*. /v/, /ɪm/
Sita*'s* got *a* pleasant manner. /z/, /ə/
D*'you* like *her*? /d/, /ə/
We *shall* come *and* see *you*. /ʃl/, /ənd/, /jʊ/
Tell *them* if you *should* see *them*. /ðəm/, /ʃəd/, /ðəm/
They*'ll* never do it. /l/
I*'d* go if I could. /d/
You can leave *at* twelve. /jʊ/, /kən/, /ət/
Curry *and* rice. /ənd/ or /ən/
Did *you* know *that the* train *was* derailed? /jʊ/, /ðət/, /ðə/, /wəz/
I wo*n't* /nt/
There*'s a* lot *to* eat. /z./ /ə/, /tʊ/
At five *to* seven. /ət/, /tə/
The same *for* all. /ðə/, /fər/
From time *to* time. /frəm/ /tə/
He ca*n't* /hɪ/, /nt/
Catch *him*. /ɪm/
She wo*n't*. /ʃhɪ/, /nt/
Watch *them*. /ðəm/
The one *that you can* see. /ðə/ /ðət/ /jʊ/ /kən/
We wo*n't* /wɪ/, /nt/
You did*n't*. /jʊ/, /nt/
Ron*'s* got *some* money. /z/, /səm/
As old *as* I am. /əz/, /əz /
Bigger *than* me. /ðən/

No weak forms should be used in stressed positions. Also the verbs and prepositions listed above do not take weak forms in the final position.

Here are some examples of the use of the strong forms of structure words when they are stressed in utterances.

A : Radha's not coming today.
B : But she told me she ˈis /ɪz/ coming.

A : Mohan is in charge of this programme.
B : But I thought ˈyou /juː/ were in charge.

A : Did you say either Shruti or Sarat will come to the music recital?
B : No. I said Shruti ˈand /ænd/ Sarat will come.

A : I give up. I can't solve this puzzle.
B : Give it another try. I'm sure you ˈcan /kæn/ solve it.

A : Here's your pen.
B : That's not ˈmine. It's ˈhers.

Here are some examples of prepositions and verbs in the final position in utterances.

Prepositions
Where does he come *from*? /frɒm/ <u>not</u> /frəm/
What are you looking *at*? /æt <u>not</u> /ət/

Verbs
He's taller than I *am*. /æm/ <u>not</u> /əm or m/
Come back as soon as you *can* /kæn/ <u>not</u> /kən/

A: *Have* you told her about it? /həv/
B : Oh yes, I *have* /hæv/ <u>not</u> /həv/

A : The problem *was* rather difficult. /wəz/
B : It certainly *was* /wɒz/ not /wəz/

8.3 Intonation

When we listen to someone speaking, we can distinguish continual variations in the levels at which the voice is pitched. In this way the speaking voice to some extent resembles the singing voice. These *intonation* patterns, as they are called, are different in different languages, but as the use of the word 'pattern' perhaps indicates, changes in vocal pitch are not haphazard. The factors that chiefly determine the choice of one pattern as against another are both objective and subjective, objective in that the type of utterance (statement vs. question, command vs. request, even simple vs. complex sentence) is important, and subjective in that the speaker's mood and his attitude to what he is saying are also significant.

Intonation can be used with great subtlety, sometimes to convey information that is not overtly expressed by the words themselves. Thus if a speaker says 'She's very beautiful' with a falling intonation, then he means precisely that; if, however, he says the same sentence with a falling-rising intonation, he probably means that although the lady in question may be beautiful, her character is defective in some other way.

Stress and intonation are linked phenomena; they work together to give the effect of 'prominence' or stress. Stressed syllables can be said with level pitch, high or low, or with a change in pitch. A stressed syllable said on level pitch is described as having a *static tone*, whilst a stressed syllable on which a pitch change takes place has a *kinetic tone*. The syllable which initiates a kinetic tone is called the *nucleus* and is said to have the primary, nuclear, or *tonic stress*. Thus the sentence

They ˈcame at ˈnight

would normally be said in British English with a high level (static) tone on *came* and a falling nucleus, or falling kinetic tone, on *night*. A more detailed classification of nuclei follows.

Another factor which affects intonation is the speaker's emotions, the degree of intensity he brings to bear on what he is saying. Generally speaking, the more a speaker is involved with what he is saying, by way of anger, grief, excitement, self-importance and so on, the greater will be the range of pitch and the amount of pitch change he uses; everyday speech, on the other hand, with little emotional content, or even fatigued speech (tiredness acting as an emotional suppressive) is said within a more limited pitch range.

It must be admitted that the system of intonation patterns used by a native speaker of English, as of any other language, is complex. A foreign learner of the language would need years of study and practice before he could use the total system with the same facility as one born to it. It is possible, however, to learn and use a simplified system which will be completely intelligible and enable the learner to avoid conveying false impressions.

The Tones
- *Level (Static)*
  - A high level tone will be marked with a symbol ' above and in front of the syllable to which it refers:

    'Those
    'Have

  - A low level tone will be marked with a symbol ₁ below and in front of the syllable to which it refers:

    ₁Now
    ₁Then

    This mark is also used to indicate stressed syllables after a falling nucleus and a mark above and in front of the stressed syllable, e.g., 'Now, 'Then, is also used after a rising nucleus.

- *Moving (Kinetic)*
  - A falling tone will be marked with a symbol ˋ in front of the syllable to which it refers. The symbol will be above the line for a high falling tone and below the line for a low falling tone.

ˈThen   ˌLook
ˈDo   ˌTell

- A rising tone will be marked with a symbol ′ in front of the syllable to which it refers. The symbol will be above the line for a high rising tone and below the line for a low rising tone.

′Yours   ˌCar
′Three   ˌThese

- A falling-rising tone will be marked with a symbol ᵛ above and in front of the syllable to which it refers.

ᵛTry
ᵛSoft
ᵛSleep

Placing the Nucleus

When a foreign learner is confronted with a passage to be read, or indeed asked to speak, the most difficult problems of intonation he has to face are where to place the nuclear tones and in what direction they should move. Correct habits have first to be learned mechanistically at the conscious level so that later the speaker can use the system instinctively.

The golden rule for the correct placing of nuclear stress is that a pitch change will very often take place on that syllable of the group (for division of an utterance into groups see the next section) which the speaker wishes to make the most *prominent*. A few examples will illustrate this point.

I ˈhate ˈwinter. (I may, however, like summer or the rainy season.)
I ˈhate ˌwinter. (I'm insisting on my emotion.)
ˈI hate ˌwinter. (Although my brother is very fond of it.)

Many utterances are of course much less dramatic than these. Some syllables may be made prominent merely to indicate completion. The speaker has either finished what he has to say and will wait for a reply, or has at least reached an intermediate conclusion and will pause for a moment before going on to say something else.

Good ˈmorning.
It's ˌsix o'ˌclock... Shall we ˌgo?

Thus if no special prominence is intended, the nucleus is on the last stressed syllable in the group.

Division into Groups

Given that a foreign learner may know that the most 'important' syllable of a group will take the nuclear accent, how is he to know what precisely constitutes a group, where it begins and where it ends?

♦ The absolute limits in the length of a group are obviously physiologically conditioned, in that no speaker can prolong a group for longer than he has breath to speak. In practice, we will prolong no group for longer than seems comfortable. Division into groups is therefore linked with breath control. In the sentence 'When I went to see them, they were out' it is natural to make a slight pause, to cut off the outgoing air stream after the word *them* and before the word *they*.

When I went to see them/they were out. (A line/is used to mark off one group from another.)

This same sentence could be said as one group, although it is less likely, and that is about as far as one could go. Any additional clause would almost inevitably lead to another group.

When I went to see them they were out,/so I went back home.

or

When I went to see them,/they were out,/so I went back home.

If we look again at the first simpler sentence, we note that the most significant word in the first group is *see* and in the second *out*. These are therefore the syllables which take the nuclear accent. A likely rendering of the sentence is:

When I ˈwent to ˌsee them, /they were ˋout/

- Punctuation, which also correlates fairly closely with breath pauses, is a useful though not infallible guide to the beginnings and ends of groups. A full stop, colon or semicolon will always mark the end of a group, and a comma usually will.

ˈEven though I've ˈnever ˇmet him, /I ˈfeel I ˈknow all aˋbout him./

- Many groups, however, can *not* be divided precisely according to punctuation marks, and then the learner must look for clues in the distribution of meaning in the utterance, or in its grammatical structure. Consider the following passage:

    There's a city in South India called Hyderabad. I shall always remember it, firstly because I lived there happily for almost two years, and secondly, because it was hotter there than at any place I'd ever been before, or have visited ever since.

In the first sentence the information about where the city is seems as important as its name. The sentence therefore has two groups.

There's a ˈcity in ˈSouth ˌIndia / called ˌHyderabad./

The first group has a rising nucleus to signify an incomplete utterance. The second has a falling nucleus. The first comma of the second sentence marks off the end of the next group, and again there is a rising tone for incomplete utterance. There are, of course, grammatical reasons for making a break here in that the main clause ends and a subordinate clause begins:

I shall ˈalways reˌmember it /...

The next group would, in British English, normally take a falling-rising nucleus on the word *years*. This helps to convey an atmosphere of warmth and the speaker's pleasure in remembering his experiences. (There might also be a falling nucleus on the word *happily*, a word important here from the point of view of meaning. This would make for a livelier reading):

...ˈfirstly because I ˈlived there (ˈ) ˈhappily for ˈalmost ˈtwo ˇyears /

In the next clause the words *there* and *before* are contrasted and made prominent and both take nuclear tones, the first falling, the second rising:

...and ˈsecondly because it was ˈhotter ˈthere /than at ˈany ˈplace I'd ˈever been beˌfore,/

The last group, making the end of the statement, takes a falling tone:

...or have ˈvisited ˈever ˈsince./

An utterance can therefore be divided into groups by noting carefully, structural and semantic clues.

Indian speakers sometimes do not divide their sentences into groups correctly. Sometimes they place the intonation nucleus on the wrong word, e.g.,

- ˈGood evening.
  (The normal English pattern is to make *evening* the nucleus.)
- ˈIn addition to ˌthis.
  (Ordinarily there would be a falling-rising nucleus on the second syllable of *addition*.)
- It is ˈfour o'clock.
  (In native English the nucleus is ordinarily on the second syllable of *o'clock*.)
- ˈI ˌdidn't /ˈask you ˈto.
  (Ordinarily there should be only one group with a falling nucleus on *ask*.)
- I ˌfared well, /I ˌthink.
  (Ordinarily the falling nucleus should be on *well*).
- ˈI know ˌwhat you mean.
  (The normal pattern would be: I ˈknow what you ˌmean)
- ᵛas far/as I ˌcould.
  (The normal pattern would be: as ˈfar as I ˌcould)
- The ˈtour ˌwas / ˈvery ˌpleasant.
  (The division should come after *tour*, not after *was*.)
- The ˈwoman ˌwas / ˌdressed / in ˈwoollens.
  (The division should come after *woman*, not after *was*.)
- I ˈwant to ˈget a ˈfew more ˈdetails from ˌyou.
  (Ordinarily the nucleus would be on *details*).

Having considered the problems of where to place nuclear stresses in an utterance, and how to divide it into groups, the question still remains of which tone to use (falling, rising or falling-rising) in a given context.

The Uses of the Tones

Falling

A falling tone is used as follows:

♦ In ordinary statements made without emotional implications:

It's ˈseven o' ˌclock.
I have a ˈlot of ˌstudents.
The ˈhouse is ˌempty.
The ˈwater's ˌwarm.

♦ In questions beginning with a question word such as *what, why* or *how,* (whose interrogative nature is therefore clear), which are said in a neutral and sometimes unfriendly way.

ˈWhy did you ˌdo it?
ˈWhen are they ˌcoming?
ˈHow will they ˌget here?
ˈWhat are they ˌmuttering about?

♦ In commands:

Do as I ˌsay.
ˈCome ˌhere.

In British R.P. the typical intonation contour of a 'tune' in which a falling tone occurs is that the first stressed syllable of the group is said on a high level note and each successive stressed syllable on a slightly lower note, until the fall on the last stressed syllable, which has the nuclear tone. Unstressed syllables, before the first stressed syllable and after a falling nuclear tone are normally said on a low note. Whether the nuclear tone takes a high or a low fall usually depends on the degree of intensity which the speaker imparts to his utterance.

Rising

The rising tone is used as follows:

- In incomplete utterances, very often as the first clause of a sentence:

    It's ˈseven o' ˌclock (but she hasn't got up yet).
    I have a ˈlot of ˌstudents (and some are quite bright).
    The ˈhouse is ˌempty (and has been for years).
    The ˈwater's ˌwarm (so why don't you come in).

Compare these sentences with the first four sentences at the beginning of this section (under the heading, 'Falling').

- In questions which demand an answer *yes* or *no*:

    ˈAre they ˌcoming?
    ˈWill you ˌdo it?
    ˈHasn't the ˈlecture ˌstarted yet?
    Have you ˈseen my ˈyounger ˌbrother?

- In questions which begin with a question word such as *what, why* or *how,* and which are said in a warm friendly manner (cf. the second set of sentences under the heading, 'Falling', above):

    ˈHow's your ˌmother?
    ˈWhy didn't you ˈcome and ˌsee me?
    ˈWhat ˌtime is it?

- In polite requests:

    ˈWould you ˈopen the ˌwindow?
    ˈPlease sit ˌdown.

As may be seen from a study of the examples above, whenever there is a *choice* between a rising and a falling tone, a rising tone indicates involvement as opposed to neutrality, friendliness as opposed to hostility.

The beginning of the intonation contour in a 'tune' in which a rising tone occurs is the same as for a falling tone, in that the first stressed syllable is said on a high level note and any following stressed syllable on successively lower notes. The last stressed syllable, having the nuclear tone, is said on a rising note, any following stressed syllables continuing the rise. Whether a rising tone goes up to mid or high pitch is again largely a matter of the degree of emotional intensity involved.

Falling - Rising

The falling-rising tone is typically used for special implications, and gives the impression that the listener should understand more than a literal interpretation of the words. Its use in statements can be contrasted with that of a falling tone, where nothing extra is meant to be read into the remarks uttered. The term 'special implication' can cover insinuation, veiled insult, apology, unpleasant news, happiness, reassurance, or doubt on the part of the speaker as to the validity of his remark. Here are some examples of the use of this tone. The fall-rise may take place on one syllable, or it may be spread over several, in which case it is referred to as 'divided'.

I'm ˈgoing there this ˇevening.	(Even though you may have expected me to go earlier, this is the best I can do.)
Iˈdidn't see you at the ˇtheatre.	(I saw you somewhere else, and you didn't realise it.)
The ˇhouses are ˌnice.	(but perhaps the people in them aren't so pleasant.)
His ˇbrother will ˌcome.	(which is just as good for our purposes, so don't worry.)
He's ˈnot as ˈstupid as I ˇthought.	(which, even though he's still quite stupid, is a good thing.)
ˈDo it at ˌonce.	(I know that a person of your type won't do it unless I tell him to.)

9. Factors Affecting the International Intelligibility of Indian English and Suggestions for Improvement

9.1 Features that Affect the Intelligibility of Indian English

It has been found[1] that the following features in Indian English are the most frequent causes of its being unintelligible to speakers of other varieties of English.

- Accent on the wrong syllable of a word

Examples:

Word	Pronounced as	Understood as
suitable (is not suitable for the laboratory…)	[suˈtɛbl]	the level
rendered (… they have rendered for the whole country)	[rɛnˈdʌrd]	endured / endowed

---

[1]Bansal, R.K. *The Intelligibility of Indian English*, Monograph No. 4, Second (abridged) edition, English and Foreign Languages University (earlier known as Central Institute of English and Foreign Language), Hyderabad, 1976.

Word	Pronounced as	Understood as
Richard (Richard fell rather badly...)	[rɪˈtʃaːrd]	the child
hesitate (I hesitate for a while)	[hɛdzɪˈteːt]	had a...
prefer	{ [ˈprɪfər] { [ˈprefər]	fearful briefer
character	[kæˈrektər]	{ director { corrected
decay	[ˈdɪke]	ticket
grimaces	[ˈgrɪmsɛz]	glimpses
defence	[ˈdɪfɛns]	difference
atmosphere	[ɛtˈmɒsfie]	must fear

Word ordinarily accented in connected speech left unaccented; this is often accompanied with a *very close juncture* with the preceding or the following accented word.

Examples

several other	[ˈsɛʊrləd̪ər] (no stress on *other*)	similar
Central Institute	[ˈsɛntrəlɪnstʃʊt] (no stress on *Institute*)	—
Arts College	[ˈatskɒlɪdʒ] (no stress on *College*)	—

Substitution of [d̪] for English /ð/

Examples

themselves (talking among themselves)	[ˈd̪ɛmzɛlʊz]	damsels

though	[d̪əʊ]	—
they	[d̪e]	day
these	[d̪iz]	—

Substitution of [ʊ] or [ʊʰ] for English /v/

Examples

Word	Pronounced as	Understood as
novel	[nɒʊɛl]	oral
even	[ˈɪʊn]	in
love and... (love and service)	[ˈlʌʊʰən...]	longer
twelve	[twɛlʊ]	dwell
veil	[ʊeːl]	whale / wail
vehicle	[ˈʊʌhɪkəl]	welcome

Substitution of [ʊ] for English /w/

Examples

west	[ʊɛst]	vest
where	[ʊɛər]	—
want	[ʊant]	—
what	[ʊat]	—

Wrong Usage

Examples

When as early back...	went as far back
I fed up with their...	I followed the
rather experts	by their experience
(Quite a few people were engaged, rather experts)	

Use of short [e] for R.P. /eɪ/
Examples

Words	Pronounced as	Understood as
paint	[pent]	felt
they have..	[d̪ehɛv]	the ...
natives	[ˈnetɪʊz]	nephews
train	[tren]	kin
A grade	[ˈegred]	a grade

Elision of one or more syllables
Examples

associated	[ɛsˈʃjeːtɛd]	stated
botany	[ˈbɒːtnɪ]	about me
assistant	[ˈʌstɛnt]	—
institute	[ɪnstʃut]	—
hereditary	[ˈhɛrɪterɪ]	inherited

Use of unaspirated /p/, /t/, /k/ at the beginning of accented syllables
Examples

touch	[tʌtʃ]	Dutch
teeth	[tiːt̪ʰ]	deed
tests	[tɛsts]	{ desks { deaths
requests	[rɪˈkʊɛs]	regress
twelve	[twɛlʊ]	dwell
train	[treːn]	drain
keys	[kiːs]	geese
pull	[pʊl]	bull
pack	[pæk]	back
cot	[kɔt]	got

Uncommon usage
Examples

Word	Pronounced as	Understood as
I go with them.		I work with them.
I was working actually with them.		I was welcome to live with them.
Primary schools are limited upto fifth class.		Primary schools .... up to fifth class.
You can get MBBS seat or engineering seat according to your will and pleasure.		You can get...

Mistakes in reading; substitution of another word, insertion of a word, omission of an inflectional suffix.

Examples

Marjorie wanted one too	Marjorie wanted me one too	Marjorie wanted me to
weathers	weather	—
illnesses	illness	—
fortnight	two night	—
cup	cap	—
fans	fan	—
lock	look	—
needn't	didn't	—

Substitution of [s] for /z/ in inflectional suffixes

Examples

fans (Let's get some new fans.)	[fæns]	fence

peas (Let's have some peas.)	[pi:s]	peace
knees (His knees got hurt.)	[ni:s]	niece
fears	[fɪərs]	fierce
keys	[ki:s]	geese
	[kɪs]	kiss

Choice by the listener of a word that is more likely in the context

Examples

Word	Pronounced as	Understood as
lock (His lock wasn't very good.)	[lɒ:k]	luck
hut (John hasn't even a hut).	[hʌt]	hat
guards (It all depends on the guards).	[ga:dz]	gods

Substitution of [tʰ] or [t] for English /θ/

Examples

three	[t̪ʰri:] [t̪ri:]	tree
teeth	[ti:t̪ʰ]	teat, teak, deed, deep
thin	[t̪ʰɪn] [t̪ɪn]	tin
thought	[t̪ʰɔ:t] [t̪ʰɒ:t]	taught

Suggestions for improvement

The following suggestions are offered for improving the efficiency of Indian English and making it internationally intelligible:

- The correct patterns of English word stress should be maintained.
- The correct patterns of sentence stress and rhythm should be maintained.
- The consonants / θ /, / ð /, / v / and / w / should be acquired.
- In vocabulary and syntax the normal usage should be observed.
- English vowels and diphthongs should be given correct length. If Indian / e: / and / o: / are used for R.P. / eɪ / and / əʊ /, they should be sufficiently long.
- There should be no elision of syllables.
- The voiceless plosives / p /, / t /, / k / should be aspirated at the beginning of stressed syllables.
- The reading of a set text should be done carefully with proper grouping of words and avoiding substitutions and omissions.
- The correct distribution of / s / and / z / in inflectional suffixes should be maintained.
- The correct distribution of English vowels and consonants should be learnt by the constant use of a pronouncing dictionary.

Part II
Exercises for Practice

10. Vowels

Words and sentences for practising English vowels*

1. / iː / as in <u>these.</u> (See Section 5.4.1)
    a. s<u>ea</u>t
    b. f<u>ee</u>t
    c. gr<u>ie</u>f
    d. l<u>ea</u>ves
    e. fr<u>ee</u>
    f. reˈl<u>ie</u>ve
    g. deˈc<u>ei</u>t
    h. conˈc<u>ea</u>l
    i. ˈr<u>e</u>gion
    j. ˌabsenˈt<u>ee</u>
    k. ˈBr<u>ea</u>the ˈd<u>ee</u>p before you ˌsp<u>ea</u>k.
    l. ˈCoughs and ˈsn<u>ee</u>zes ˈspread diˋs<u>ea</u>ses.
    m. The ˈtrain ˈl<u>ea</u>ves at ˈthr<u>ee</u>-ˌthirty.
    n. We ˈn<u>ee</u>d maˌch<u>i</u>nes/and we ˈn<u>ee</u>d maˈchine ˋoperators.
    o. ˈGandhij<u>i</u> saw ˈnothing unˈs<u>ee</u>mly in a ˋsw<u>ee</u>per's, ˌjob.
    p. ˈSh<u>ee</u>la ˈplayed an ˈ<u>e</u>vening ˈraga on the ˌv<u>ee</u>na.
    q. The ˈf<u>ie</u>lds get ˈgr<u>ee</u>ner and ˈgr<u>ee</u>ner in the ˋrainy ˌs<u>ea</u>son.
    r. The ˈlawyer ˈwanted his ˈf<u>ee</u>s before acˈcepting the ˌbr<u>ie</u>f.
    s. ˈCh<u>ee</u>se ˈmade from ˇgoats' ˌmilk/is ˈbetter than ˈch<u>ee</u>se ˈmade from ˋsheep's ˌmilk.
    t. ˈF<u>ee</u>lings of both ˈgr<u>ie</u>f and reˇl<u>ie</u>f/s<u>ee</u>mˋnormal on ˌsuch an ocˌcasion.

---

*In the practice materials for each vowel, the letters underlined represent that vowel.

2. /ɪ/ as in bit (See Section 5.4.2)
   a. six
   b. fit
   c. clip
   d. ridge
   e. ink
   f. ˈflimsy
   g. ˈirriˌtate
   h. ilˈicit
   i. ˌpoliˈtician
   j. reˈfrigeˌrator

   k. The ˈeggs are ˌfinished.
   l. Irriˈgation is esˈsential in this ˌcountry.
   m. ˈSixty ruˈpees if you ˈfix it ˌquickly!
   n. ˈFill it ˌin / and ˈthen ˌpost it.
   o. ˈIndia's ˈseas and ˈrivers are ˈrich in ˌfish.
   p. The Rig-ˈVeda is an ˈearly ˈSanskrit ˌtext.
   q. We'll ˈstick to him through ˈthick and ˌthin.
   r. I've had ˈchicken with ˈchillies ˈsix times this ˌweek.
   s. ˈKuchpudi ˈdancing is only ˈone of ˈmany ˌdance ˌforms.
   t. The ofˈficial ˈlanguages of the ˈUnion of ˌIndia / are ˈHindi and ˌEnglish.

3. Indian English / e: /
   British R.P. / ei / as in gate (See Section 5.4.3)
   a. save
   b. nail
   c. lame
   d. gain
   e. bathe
   f. ˈaged
   g. ˈbaker
   h. aˈfraid
   i. ˈtapeworm
   j. forˈsaken

   k. ˈSay you'll ˈstay to ˌday.
   l. ˈTake a ˈpiece of ˌcake.
   m. The ˈchild made a ˈpaper ˌplane.
   n. The ˈtrain was ˈlate ˈleaving the ˋstation.
   o. ˈShakespeare's ˈplays are supˈposed to be ˌgreat.
   p. ˈYour face has the ˋsame ˌpale ˌlook.
   q. We ˈfailed to ˈsail beˈcause of the ˌgale.

r. He be'h**a**ved in the 'same 'w**ay** as a ˌb**a**by.
s. 'Don't 'bl**a**me me if the 'games are 'badly arˌr**a**nged.
t. I'get it from the 's**a**me 'tr**a**der as my ˌn**eigh**bour.

4. British R.P./e/
   Indian English / ɛ / as in <u>bed.</u> (See Section 5.4.4)
   a. **e**dge   f. 'ch**e**mical
   b. r**e**st   g. '**e**very
   c. b**e**d   h. '**a**ny
   d. b**e**nds   i. 'l**ei**sure
   e. br**ea**th   j. 'g**e**neˌrator
   k. 'Ram's my 'b**e**st ˌfr**ie**nd.
   l. The 't**e**sts are in e'l**e**ven ˌweeks.
   m. It g**e**ts 'cooler in No'v**e**mber and Deˌc**e**mber.
   n. We 'g**e**nerate our 'own elect'ricity to ˎsome exˌt**e**nt.
   o. Her 'dr**e**ss was a 'd**e**licate 'shade of ˌy**e**llow.
   p. ʻY**e**s', said the ˌm**e**mber, / ʻI 'come '**e**very ˌW**e**dnesday'.
   q. You 'can't 'r**e**st if you 'want to get aˌh**ea**d.
   r. 'S**e**ven ᵛh**e**n ˌ**e**ggs / and 't**e**n ᵛduck **e**ggs / were ˌrotten.
   s. We 'sp**e**nd 'h**ea**vily on deˌf**e**nce /but it 'seems ˌn**e**cessary.
   t. The 'W**e**st 'End Hoˌt**e**l / is 'quite w**e**ll ˎknown in Mumˌbai.

5. / æ / as in <u>bad.</u> (See Section 5.4.5)
   a. b**a**ck   f. 'c**a**ttle
   b. fl**a**g   g. 'm**a**ngo
   c. s**a**nd   h. at't**a**ck
   d. **a**xe   j. 'gr**a**dual
   e. r**a**nk   j. '**a**ntelope
   k. 'T**a**nks de'cided ˎthat ˌb**a**ttle.

l. 'Have you got a ˌcash-box?
m. That man's a 'bad ˌworker.
n. He has 'black 'hats in his ˌbag.
o. We need 'dams and 'barrages on this ˌriver.
p. Have you 'bought a 'ticket for the 'charity ˌraffle?
q. The 'cafe's round the 'back of the ˌpark.
r. The 'taxi 'rattled as it 'ran over the ˌbumps.
s. The 'track ran 'up to a 'crack in the ˌrock.
t. I'll 'catch you at the 'back if I ˌcan.

6. British R. P.   / ʌ / ⎫
   Indian English / ə / ⎭ as in bus. (See Section 5.4.6)

   a. bl<u>oo</u>d
   b. c<u>o</u>me
   c. 'b<u>u</u>ndle
   d. 'b<u>u</u>tter
   e. 'c<u>ou</u>ntry
   f. 'c<u>ou</u>ple

   g. He 'hasn't e'n<u>ou</u>gh ˌm<u>o</u>ney.
   h. His 'tr<u>ou</u>bles are 'yet to ˌc<u>o</u>me.
   i. Please 'put this 'b<u>u</u>ndle on the ˌb<u>u</u>s.
   j. 'What 's<u>u</u>bjects do you 'wish to ˌst<u>u</u>dy?
   k. 'Get me a 'b<u>u</u>n and a 'c<u>u</u>p of ˌtea.

7. Indian English / a: / ⎫
   British R.P.   / ɑ: / ⎭ as in card. (See Section 5.4.7)

   a. h<u>a</u>lf   f. 'r<u>a</u>ther
   b. b<u>a</u>th   g. 'pl<u>a</u>ster
   c. p<u>a</u>rt   h. a'gh<u>a</u>st
   d. ch<u>a</u>rm   i. a'l<u>a</u>rm
   e. bl<u>a</u>st   j. di's<u>a</u>ster

   k. The 'armies 'marched ˌon.
   l. The 'darting 'dog a'larmed the ˌcalves.

m. My ˈgrandfaˌther has a ˈbad ˌheart.
n. ˈFather ˈneeds ˈspare ˈparts for his ˌcar.
o. ˈRam can ˈrun ˈfarther and ˈfaster than ˌyou.
p. The ˈdrought was a diˈsaster for the ˌfarmers.
q. You ˈcan't have a ˈparty in the ˌgarage.
r. He's a ˈguardian in our ˈlargest ˈNational ˌPark.
s. We were ˈrather aˈlarmed when the ˈplaster fell ˌdown.
t. The ˈfilm-star ᵛcharmed the proˌducer / into ˈgiving her the ˌpart.

8. / ɒ / as in hot. (See Section 5.4.8)
   a. not
   b. box
   c. off
   d. bond
   e. top
   f. ˈbottle
   g. ˈfollow
   h. ˈmodel
   i. reˈvolve
   j. disˈhonest
   k. ˈSalt disˈsolves in ˌwater.
   l. ˈPut your ˋsocks on, ˌRam.
   m. ˈCross me ˈoff your ˌlist.
   n. They ˈrobbed the ˈbank and ˈgot aˋway.
   o. The ˈcost of ˈcloth has gone ˌup.
   p. The ˈchild ˈtoppled ˈoff the ˈox's ˌback.
   q. ˋI wasn't at the ˌoffice / but ˈhe ˌwas.
   r. The ˈhot weather is ˈended by the monˌsoon.
   s. I ˈsaw a ˈcrocodile on a ˈlog in the ˌriver.
   t. You need a ᵛlot of ˌoxygen, / at the ˈtop of ˌEverest.

9. a. British R.P.   / ɔː / } as in all. (See Section 5.4.9)
       Indian English   / ɒ /
    i. all
    ii. exˈhaust
    iii. call
    iv. bought
    v. law

vi. c<u>au</u>se
vii. w<u>a</u>lk

viii. I ˈsaw ˌhim/ and his ˈsister ˌalso.
ix. They ˈfought in the ˈcause of ˌfreedom.
x. My ˈdaughter has ˈgone for a ˌwalk.
xi. Please ˈcall at the ˈlaundry on your ˈway ˌhome.
xii. I have ˈbought all the ˈlaw books Iˌneed.

b. British R.P. / ɔː / } as in <u>horse</u>
   Indian English / ɒr / } (See Section 5.4.9)

i. c<u>or</u>n
ii. f<u>or</u>m
iii. h<u>or</u>se
iv. n<u>or</u>th
v. <u>or</u>
vi. sh<u>or</u>t
vii. ˈm<u>or</u>ning

viii. ˈF<u>or</u>ty ˈh<u>or</u>semen were ˈgoing ˌn<u>or</u>thwards.
ix. He ˈmade a ˈf<u>or</u>tune as a ˌc<u>or</u>n merchant.
x. I have ˈmilk and ˌc<u>or</u>nflakes / for ˈbreakfast every ˌm<u>or</u>ning.
xi. He is the ˈright s<u>or</u>t of ˌman/to ˈ<u>or</u>ganise such a ˌproject.
xii. My office is ˈnot in the ˌN<u>or</u>th ˌBlock; /it is ˈjust ˈround the ˌc<u>or</u>ner.

c. British R.P. / ɔː / } as in <u>force.</u>
   Indian English / oːr / } (See Section 5.4.9)

i. f<u>or</u>ce
ii. c<u>our</u>t
iii. p<u>our</u>
iv. m<u>or</u>e
v. d<u>oor</u>

vi. Please ˈbuy some ˈfl<u>oo</u>r ˌb<u>oa</u>rd.
vii. The ˈburglars ˈf<u>o</u>rced the ˈd<u>oo</u>r ˌopen.
viii. The ˈC<u>ou</u>rt apˈpeared to be in ˈm<u>ou</u>rning.
ix. There were ˈnew ˈlands ˌlying bef<u>o</u>re the exˌpl<u>o</u>rer.
x. Shall I ˈpour some ˈmore ˌtea for you?

10. Indian English / oː /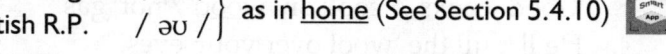
    British R.P.   / əʊ /   as in h<u>o</u>me (See Section 5.4.10)

   a. b<u>oa</u>t   f. ˈb<u>o</u>gie
   b. h<u>o</u>me   g. ˈ<u>o</u>pen
   c. b<u>o</u>th   h. ˈc<u>oa</u>stal
   d. b<u>oa</u>st   i. ˈgh<u>o</u>stly
   e. g<u>o</u>ld   j. reˈv<u>o</u>lting

   k. ˈBl<u>ow</u> your ˌn<u>o</u>se.
   l. This ˈt<u>oa</u>st's ˌc<u>o</u>ld.
   m. We unˈl<u>oa</u>ded the ˈb<u>oa</u>ts toˌday.
   n. ˈD<u>o</u>n't ˈg<u>o</u> toˌday, / ˈg<u>o</u> to ˈmorrow.
   o. ˈL<u>oa</u>d the ˈtruck with ˌc<u>oa</u>l.
   p. ˈThr<u>ow</u> that ˈ<u>o</u>ld ˈb<u>o</u>ne to the ˌdog.
   q. I'll ˈsh<u>ow</u> it you in your ˈ<u>ow</u>n ˌh<u>o</u>me.
   r. I'm ˈg<u>o</u>ing to play a ˈj<u>o</u>ke on the ˌp<u>o</u>stman.
   s. The ˈv<u>o</u>ting in Hiˈmachal Praˌdesh / was p<u>o</u>stˈp<u>o</u>ned because of ˌsn<u>ow</u>.
   t. Your ˈc<u>oa</u>t's ˈvery ˌ<u>o</u>ld / and there's a ˈh<u>o</u>le in your ˌdh<u>o</u>ti.

11. / ʊ / as in b<u>oo</u>k (See Section 5.4.11)

   a. f<u>u</u>ll   f. ˈc<u>u</u>shion
   b. sh<u>ou</u>ld   g. ˈb<u>u</u>tcher
   c. w<u>oo</u>d   h. ˈcr<u>oo</u>ked
   d. b<u>oo</u>k   i. ˈb<u>u</u>llet
   e. p<u>u</u>t   j. ˈb<u>u</u>shes

k. You've ˈput your ˌfoot in it.
l. You ˈhaven't underˈstood the ˌbook.
m. We'd ˈuse ˈwood if we ˌcould.
n. ˈDo ˈgood to ˌall.
o. You ˈshouldn't wear ˈwool in ˌsummer.
p. She's a ˈnice-looking ˌwoman.
q. ˈGive it a ˈgoodˈ ˌpull.
r. ˈGood ˌcooks / ˈcook on ˌwood /ˈnot ˌgas.
s. He'll ˈpull the ˈwool over your ˌeyes.
t. By ˈhook or by ˌcrook / I'll ˈget through this ˌbook.

12. / uː / as in <u>rule</u>, <u>tube</u>. (See Section 5.4.12)

    a. t<u>u</u>be   f. apˈpr<u>o</u>ve
    b. r<u>u</u>le   g. ˈbr<u>ui</u>ses
    c. gr<u>oo</u>ve   h. ˈf<u>oo</u>lish
    d. s<u>ui</u>t   i. ˈcr<u>ui</u>ser
    e. l<u>oo</u>m   j. ˈm<u>u</u>sic

k. Y<u>ou</u>'ll ˈl<u>o</u>se if you ˌs<u>ue</u> me.
l. You're a ˈf<u>oo</u>lish ˈstupid ˌy<u>ou</u>th.
m. She's the most ˈb<u>eau</u>tiful ˈp<u>u</u>pil in the ˌgr<u>ou</u>p.
n. We'll ˈm<u>o</u>ve to Bomˈbay if it ˌs<u>ui</u>ts us.
o. The monˈs<u>oo</u>n came unˈ<u>u</u>sually ˌlate that ˌJune.
p. Did ˌy<u>ou</u> ˌch<u>oo</u>se the ˌm<u>u</u>sic?
q. Will I ˈl<u>o</u>se your apˌpr<u>o</u>val?
r. There's a ˈrare ˈbl<u>ue</u> ˈg<u>oo</u>se at the ˌz<u>oo</u>.
s. I'd ˈs<u>oo</u>ner ˈl<u>o</u>se a ˈfew r<u>u</u>ˈpees than ˈd<u>o</u> ˌthat.
t. D<u>o</u> y<u>ou</u> use ˈr<u>u</u>lers at ˌsch<u>oo</u>l?

13. British R.P.   / ɜː /
    Indian English / ər /   as in <u>serve</u> (See Section 5.4.13)

    a. b<u>ir</u>d
    b. b<u>ur</u>n
    c. w<u>or</u>d
    d. ˈ<u>ear</u>ly

e. ˈjourney
f. There's a ˈgirl beˈhind that ˌcurtain.
g. The ˈworld situˈation is ˈgetting ˌworse.
h. It is a ˈperfect ˈwork of ˌart.
i. ˈTry to ˈlearn as ˈmany new ˈwords as ˌpossible.
j. ˈEven though I'm ˌthirsty, /1 ˈcan't ˈdrink this ˈdirty ˌwater.

14. / ə / as in { acˈcount (first syllable), ˈhuman (second syllable), (See Section 5.4.14) }

a. aˈbout
b. ˈfather
c. ˈhuman
d. ˈbackward
e. ˈdoctor
f. ˈribbon
g. ˈpicture
h. conˈtrol
i. conˈnect
j. reˈfrigerator
k. I reˈturned at about ˈthree oˈˌclock.
l. Please ˈenter this in the ac ˌcount.
m. My ˈfather was ˈformerly a ˌminister.
n. I have ˈno conˈtrol over them.
o. My ˈelder ˈbrother is a ˌdoctor.
p. These ˈanimals are in ˈvery ˈgood conˌdition.
q. She is ˈnot conˈnected with this afˌfair.
r. My asˈsistant will deˈliver it at ˈten oˈˌclock.
s. The ˈweather's ˈcooler in Deˈcember than in ˌJune.
t. The ˈbank will ˌpay you / ˈfour and a ˈhalf perˈcent ˌinterest.

15. / aɪ / as in bite. (See Section 5.4.16)

a. crime
b. bright
c. die
d. sigh
f. ˈliar
g. ˈtiger
h. reˈsign
i. ˌoutˈside

e. fl<u>y</u>
j. re'v<u>i</u>val
k. You must 'sign 'f<u>i</u>ve ˌtimes.
l. It's a 'very 'f<u>i</u>ne deˌsign.
m. The 'bright 'sunl<u>i</u>ght 'dazzles my ˌ<u>ey</u>es.
n. He ˌs<u>igh</u>ed, / 'cr<u>ied</u> ˌout / and then ˌd<u>ied</u>.
o. 'When <u>I</u> 'tell ˌl<u>ies</u>/ <u>I</u> 'sm<u>i</u>le ˌn<u>i</u>cely.
p. The 'p<u>i</u>lot 'didn't fl<u>y</u> ˈh<u>igh</u> that ˌtime.
q. 'B<u>uy</u> me an 'ice-'cream or <u>I</u>'ll ˌcr<u>y</u>.
r. <u>I</u>'ll 'wr<u>i</u>te my 'book in a 'f<u>i</u>ne ˌst<u>y</u>le.
s. The 'ch<u>i</u>ld ˌthought / he 'could cl<u>i</u>mb as 'h<u>igh</u> as the ˌsk<u>y</u>.
t. We 'd<u>i</u>ne at ˌeight / and then 'listen to the 'radio for 'some ˌt<u>i</u>me.

16. / ɔɪ / as in b<u>oi</u>l (See Section 5.4.17)

a. t<u>oy</u>
b. b<u>oi</u>l
c. n<u>oi</u>se
d. j<u>oi</u>n
e. j<u>oy</u>
f. 'l<u>oi</u>ter
g. 'b<u>oy</u>ish
h. em'pl<u>oy</u>
i. ex'pl<u>oi</u>t
j. dis'j<u>oi</u>nted

k. Jag'dish 'j<u>oi</u>ned an ˈ<u>oi</u>l ˌcompany.
l. It was 'sp<u>oi</u>lt by ˌm<u>oi</u>sture.
m. The 'house ad'j<u>oi</u>ning was desˌtr<u>oy</u>ed,
n. The 'poor 't<u>oi</u>lers were exˌpl<u>oi</u>ted.
o. He's a 'n<u>oi</u>sy, 'b<u>oi</u>sterous ˌb<u>oy</u>.
p. We'll em'pl<u>oy</u> a 'stoker for the ˌb<u>oi</u>ler.
q. We a'v<u>oi</u>d 't<u>oi</u>l if we 'have any ˌch<u>oi</u>ce.
r. She 'paints very 'well in ˌ<u>oi</u>ls.
s. "Have you an apˌp<u>oi</u>ntment?' she ˌsaid in a ˌc<u>oy</u>ˌ v<u>oi</u>ce.
t. I've 'b<u>oi</u>ls on my ˌneck / and 'stiffness in my ˌj<u>oi</u>nts.

Vowels

17. Indian English / aʊ / ⎫
    British R.P.   /au/ ⎭ as in house, (See Section 5.4.18)

    a. d**ow**n
    b. c**ow**
    c. h**ow**l
    d. b**ou**nd
    e. d**ou**bt
    f. ˈv**ow**el
    g. ˈc**ow**ard
    h. aˈr**ou**nd
    i. reˈb**ou**nding
    j. deˈv**ou**ring

    k. The ˈcr**ow**d ˈh**ow**led ˌl**ou**dly.
    l. He ˈfr**ow**ned at my ˌd**ou**bts.
    m. We ˈwalked r**ou**nd the ˈt**ow**n ˌb**ou**ndaries.
    n. Can you proˈn**ou**nce this ˌv**ow**el ˌs**ou**nd?
    o. The ˈ**ow**l gazed ˈd**ow**n at the ˌc**ow**.
    p. ˈSomewhere ab**ou**t the ˈh**ou**se there's a ˌm**ou**se.
    q. ˈPl**ou**ghing is ˈeasier to the ˋs**ou**th of the ˌm**ou**ntain.
    r. The ˈhens were ˈchirping ˈdr**ow**sily in the ˌf**ow**l ˌh**ou**se.
    s. I ˈalmost ˌdr**ow**ned / and was aˈst**ou**nded when Iˈ came aˌr**ou**nd.
    t. The ˈtiger ˋgr**ow**led, / ˈpawed the ˋgr**ou**nd, / and ˈthen ˌb**ou**nded at me.

18. / ɪə / as in cheer. (See Section 5.4.19)

    a. m**e**re
    b. h**e**re
    c. j**ee**r
    d. f**ea**r
    e. d**ea**r
    f. caˈr**ee**r
    g. seˈv**e**re
    h. ˈcl**ea**ring
    I. apˈp**ea**r
    j. ˈcur**iou**s

    k. We ˈf**ea**r she's disapˌp**ea**red.
    l. They ˈj**ee**red the ˌch**ee**r-leader.
    m. ˈWipe away your ˌt**ea**rs, ˌd**ea**r.
    n. ˈYours is aˋqu**ee**r caˌr**ee**r!
    o. ˈThings get ˈd**ea**rer and ˈd**ea**rer every ˌy**ea**r.
    p. Weˈr**e** ˈno ˈn**ea**rer the ˌp**ie**r ˌh**e**re.

q. My 'mother-in-law's a 'hid<u>eou</u>s 'old interˏf<u>e</u>rer.
r. The 'natives have 'p<u>ie</u>rced ˏ<u>ea</u>rs / and 'carry ˏsp<u>ea</u>rs.
s. He 'grew a 'w<u>ei</u>rd ˏb<u>ea</u>rd/ to 'hide his 'meek exˏt<u>e</u>rior.
t. The 'd<u>ee</u>r in this ˏpark / do 'not 'f<u>ea</u>r to 'come n<u>ea</u>r the ˏvisitors.

19. Indian English / eə / ⎫
    British R.P. / ɛə / ⎭ as in <u>air</u> (See Sectlon 5.4.20)

   a. ch<u>ai</u>r   f. a'w<u>a</u>re
   b. r<u>a</u>re   g. af'f<u>ai</u>r
   c. sc<u>a</u>rce   h. 't<u>ea</u>ring
   d. wh<u>e</u>re   i. 'd<u>a</u>ring
   e. b<u>ea</u>r   j. 'sc<u>a</u>rcely

   k. 'Wh<u>e</u>re's the 'r<u>a</u>re ˏb<u>ea</u>r?
   l. 'Sita will 't<u>ea</u>r your ˏh<u>ai</u>r out!
   m. I can 'b<u>a</u>rely 'sp<u>a</u>re the ˏtime.
   n. I'm 'sc<u>a</u>rcely aˋw<u>a</u>re of the afˏf<u>ai</u>r.
   o. Th<u>e</u>re's a 'ch<u>ai</u>r below the ˏst<u>ai</u>rs.
   p. How ˋd<u>a</u>re you ˎmeddle in my afˏf<u>ai</u>rs?
   q. The 'm<u>a</u>re ˏst<u>a</u>red at us / and we 'st<u>a</u>red ˏback.
   r. It will be 'quite 'f<u>ai</u>r if we 'sh<u>a</u>re the exˏpenses.
   s. The 'loud-'speakers are 'bl<u>a</u>ring in the ˏsqu<u>a</u>re / 'every 'time I'm ˏth<u>e</u>re.
   t. So 'long as he can pre'p<u>a</u>re my ᵛfood ˎproperly, I'm happy.

20. / uə / as in <u>poor.</u> (See Section 5.4.21)

   a. p<u>oo</u>r   c. 'act<u>u</u>al
   b. s<u>ew</u>er   d. 'virt<u>uou</u>s

   e. 'Act<u>ua</u>lly he is 'very ˏp<u>oo</u>r.
   f. 'These 'men are 'quite suˏperfl<u>uou</u>s.
   g. There's 'no ˋf<u>ue</u>l aˎvailable ˎhere.

h. The ˈreasons for the ˌduel / were ˈnot ˏknown.
i. We ˈwant some ˈvirt<u>uou</u>s ˈmen to ˈtake it ˏup.

Words and sentences for practising vowel contrasts

1. /iː/ — /ɪ/

/iː/	/ɪ/
a. seat	sit
b. heal	hill
c. dean	din
d. reach	rich
e. green	grin
f. beads	bids
g. meals	mills
h. ease	is
i. ˈbeaten	ˈbitten
j. ˈbeaches	ˈbitches

k. We ˈeach ˈcaught ˈfifty ˏfish.
l. It's a bit ˈgreasy for me.
m. ˈFeel the ˈthickness of the ˏcloth.
n. We'll ˈreach the ˈbeach in a ˋlittle ˌbit.
o. ˈDon't drink a ˈlot of ˈwater with ˏmeals.
p. ˈPlease beˈlieve him when he ˈsays he's ˏill.
q. You can ˈfeel the ˈwind from the ˏhills.
r. It's ˈnot ˈeasy to get ˈrich ˏquickly.
s. She was ˈbitten by a ˌleech / but it'll ˏheal.
t. Did you ˈknow he ˌgrinned as he ˌbeat me?

Some Assamese, Bengali, Bihari Hindi, Gujarati, Marathi and Odiya speakers have difficulty with this contrast.

2. /iː/ — { Indian English /eː/
British R.P. /eɪ/ }

/iː/	Indian English /eː/ R.P. /eɪ/
a. meal	mail
b. kneel	nail
c. seal	sail
d. heal	hail
e. teak	take
f. meek	make
g. sheep	shape
h. feet	fate
i. ˈbeaker	ˈbaker
j. ˈgreeted	ˈgrated

k. ˈPlay the ˈsame ˈscene aˌgain.
l. There's ˈno esˈcape from the ˌheat.
m. The ˈfailure ˈrate inˈcreased this ˌyear.
n. ˈEach ˈcrate is ˈmade of ˌteak.
o. Some ˈsleep will ˈmake you feel ˌbetter.
p. I ˈgrazed my ˈheel on a ˌnail.
q. It'll ˈtake a ˈfew ˈdays to ˌheal.
r. I'll ˈmake them ˌkneel at my ˌfeet some ˌday.
s. The ˈwheel is ˈone of the ˈsymbols of ˌfate.
t. ˈSome people would be ˈgrateful for ˌtwo meals a ˌday.

3. /iː/ — /əɪ/

/iː/	British R.P. /ɪə/ Indian English / ɪər /
a. bead	beard
b. fee	fear
c. bee	beer

d. see seer
e. tea tier
f. he here
g. me mere
h. we weir
i. knee near
j. pea pier

k. ˈExcellent ˈtea is ˈgrown near ˌhere.
l. We're ˈstruggling to ˈmeet the ˌfees.
m. ˈChanging ˈgear will ˈseem ˌeasy.
n. We reˈvered him as a ˈgreat ˌleader.
o. We'll ˈsee about ˈcamping gear in Darˌjeeling.
p. I ˈtravelled in a ˈthree-tier ˌsleeping-ˌcar.
q. I beˈlieve their ˈgoods are ˈvery ˌdear.
r. That'll ˈteach you ˈnot to ˈjeer at ˌpeople.
s. It ˈseems he ˈgrew the ˈbeard to ˌtease me.
t. She was a ˈmere ˌgirl/ but she reˈvealed no ˌfear.

4. /ɪ/ — {Indian English /eː/
        British R.P. /eɪ/

/ɪ/	Indian English / eː / R.P. /eɪ/
a. mill	mail
b. sill	sail
c. hill	hail
d. tick	take
e. sick	sake
f. sin	sane
g. fit	fate
h. grit	grate
i. hit	hate
j. ˈbicker	ˈbaker

k. ˈSeven ˈships ˈsailed aˌway.
l. I'm aˈfraid the ˈmills are ˌclosed toˌday.
m. Their ˈbickering would ˈdrive a ˋsaint inˌ sane.
n. We're ˈsick of the ˈsame ˈfood ˈeveryˌday
o. ˈWomen's ˈshapes ˈchange with the ˈdictates of ˌfashion.
p. I ˈhit him ˈsix ˌtimes / because Iˌhate him.
q. The ˈmail ˈtrain was deˌrailed / ˈcoming ˈdown the inˌcline.
r. The ˈtick of the ˈclock ˈgrates on my ˌnerves.
s. The ˈriver's in a ˈdangerous ˋstate / since the ˌrains.
t. If you ˈgive me the ˈsame ˌthing, / I ˈwon'tˌpay.

5. /ɪ/ — { British R.P. /e/
         Indian English /ɛ/

/ɪ/	R.P. /e/ Indian English / ɛ /
a. will	well
b. tin	ten
c. mint	meant
d. rich	wretch
e. sit	set
f. hid	head
g. trick	trek
h. miss	mess
i. ˈmiddle	ˈmeddle
j. ˈbitter	ˈbetter

k. The ˈwelding ˈisn't sufˈficiently ˌstrong.
l. They're ˈseventy-ˈsix and ˈfifty-ˈseven resˌpectively.
m. ˈTell me which is the ˌbest.
n. We've had eˈnough of your ˌmeddling ˌtricks.

o. They've ˈno ˈsense of ˈguilt or ˌsin.
p. The ˈtents were ˈripped by the ˌwind.
q. His efˈficiency has made him a ˈwealthy ˌman.
r. You ˈleft things in a ˈbit of a ˌmess, ˌMiss.
s. We comˈmemorated his ˈdeath in the ˈmiddle of the ˌmonth.
t. We got ˈtwenty-ˈsix chickens / but the ˈrest of the ˈeggs were ˌaddled.

6. Indian English /e:/ — /ɛ/
   British R.P.   /eɪ/ — /e/

Indian English / e: / R.P./eɪ/	Indian English / ɛ / R.P./e/
a. main	men
b. saint	sent
c. hail	hell
d. fail	fell
e. wail	well
f. spade	sped
g. raid	red
h. sale	sell
i. wait	wet
j. ˈlater	ˈletter

k. That ˈegg ˈcurry ˈtastes ˌtainted.
l. Does it ˈever ˈrain in Sepˌtember?
m. The ˈracing-boat ˈsped over the ˌwaves.
n. ˈMany men ˈclaim Viˈnobaji as a ˌsaint.
o. The ˈother ˈpainter's ˈjealous of my ˌreds.
p. The exˈtent of our ˈforeign ˈtrade is ˌspreading.
q. ˈMany ˈwomen were ˈwailing after the ˌair-raid.
r. I'd have ˈfailed had ˈI been ˈsent as ˌwell.
s. We ˈdidn't ˈwait for our ˈtents to ˈget any ˌwetter.
t. ˈThat place is as ˈhot as the ˈflames of ˌhell.

Some Assamese, Bengali, Gujarati, Hindi, Kashmiri, Marathi, Odiya, Punjabi and Urdu speakers have difficulty with this contrast.

7. Indian English / e: /
   British R.P.   /eɪ/   } — /æ/

Indian English /e:/ R.P. /eɪ/	/æ/
a. main	man
b. rain	ran
c. brain	bran
d. hate	hat
e. mate	mat
f. rate	rat
g. made	mad
h. laid	lad
i. glade	glad
j. chafe	chaff

k. I 'hate 'fat ˌrats.
l. The 'lad's got ˌbrains.
m. He 'claimed the 'chain had ˌsnapped.
n. The 'rain lashed 'down on the ˌsandbanks.
o. Can you 'find a 'place for your ˌhat?
p. The 'train ran 'off the ˌrails / and ˋcrashed.
q. 'Play the 'ace of 'spades from the ˌpack.
r. We must 'save the 'maize 'crop if we ˌcan.
s. There are 'faint 'traces of ˌblood in the ˌsand.
t. I'm a'fraid the 'bank ca'shier made a'way with your ˌsavings.

Vowels

8. Indian English / e: / — / eər /
   British R.P. / eɪ / — /ɛə/

Indian English / e: / R.P. /eɪ/	Indian English / eər / R.P. /ɛə/
a. hay	hair
b. bay	bare
c. ray	rare
d. stays	stairs
e. day	dare

   f. 'Trains are 'rarely deˌrailed.
   g. 'Take that 'tray upˌstairs.
   h. We 'daren't ˌbathe ˌthere.
   i. The 'sun 'glared 'down all ˌday.
   j. I 'blame them for 'unfair ˌplay.
   k. He 'flared up in a ˌrage.
   l. May we 'go to the ˌfair toˌday?
   m. The 'mare 'ate the ˋhay we ˌgave her.
   n. 'Indian 'women in the ˌmain / 'don't have ˋfair ˌhair.
   o. We de'clared at 'close of 'play on the 'second ˌday.

9. British R.P. /e:/
   Indian English / ɛ / } —/æ/

Indian English / e: /	/ æ /
a. men	man
b. ten	tan
c. send	sand
d. lend	land
e. guess	gas
f. mess	mass
g. bet	bat

h. bed   bad
i. ˈkettle   ˈcattle
j. ˈletter   ˈlatter

k. A ˈman must ˈfend for him ˌself.
l. We ˈguessed there'd be a ˌgas attack.
m. His ˈtent was ˈbadly eˈrected and colˌlapsed.
n. ˈSell as ˈmany ˈdaggers as you ˌcan.
o. The ˈbattle made a ˈmess of our ˌland.
p. It's ˈvery ᵛsad / but there ˈisn't any ˌbread.
q. I'll ˈbless the ˈman who ˈfetches the ˌvan.
r. I ˈmade my ˈbed in the ᵛsand / and ˋslept.
s. ˈSend for a ˈladder and get ˈon to the ˌroof.
t. There's a ˈred ˈflag on the ˌbank', he said.

Some Assamese, Bengali, Gujarati, Hindi, Kashmiri, Marathi, Odiya, Punjabi and Urdu speakers have difficulty with this contrast.

10. / æ / — { Indian English / aːr /
               British R.P. / ɑː / }

/ æ /	Indian English / aːr / R.P. / ɑː /
a. back	bark
b. cat	cart
c. hat	heart
d. pack	park

e. She ˈdoesn't ˈhalf ˈlack ˌtact.
f. The ˈpath's ˈfar from ˌflat.
g. ˈHandle the ˈvaseˌcarefully; / its ˌfragile.
h. Have you ˈseen the ˈcracks in the ˌplaster?
i. The ˈcalf got ˈbadly enˈtangled in a ˋthorn bush.
j. ˈEverything was ˈflattened in the ˈpath of the ˌstorm.

k. These ˈblackguards ˈlaughed as they ˈran ˈoff with my ˌcash?

11. British R.P.   / ʌ / ⎫
    Indian English / ə / ⎬ — / ɒ /
                          ⎭

R.P. /ʌ/ Indian English / ə /	/ɒ/
a. cut	cot
b. cuff	cough
c. lust	lost
d. tongues	tongs
e. rung	wrong

f. ˈWhat's your ˌmother ˌtongue?
g. I've got a ˈhorrible ˌcough.
h. I'm ˈnot ˈfond of ˌforeigners.
i. ˈCome up aˌloft', ˌshouted the ˌsailor.
j. He fell ˈoff the ˈtop ˌrung.
k. The ˈgutters are ˈblocked with ˌmud.
l. Have you ˈlost your ˌtongue, young ˌman?
m. He's got a ˈpositive ˈlust for ˌlife.
n. I've ˈsigned a ˈbond for my ˌscholarship.
o. He had a ˈlong ˈdeep ˈcut on his ˌforehead.

12. Indian English / a: / ⎫
    British R.P.   / ɑ: / ⎬ — /ɒ/
                          ⎭

Indian English / a: / R.P. / ɑ:/	/ɒ/
a. last	lost
b. glass	gloss
c. balm	bomb
d. glassy	ˈglossy
e. ˈfaster	ˈfoster

f. Her ˈsong techˈnique is ˌmasterly.
g. Prem ˈhasn't got a ˈlarge ˌfarm.
h. There are ˈrocks outˈside the ˌharbour.
i. The ˈplay's got a ˈlarge ˌcast.
j. Superˈficial ˈknowledge does a ˈlot of ˌharm.
k. An ˈarms ˈrace in aˈtomic ˈbombs and ˌrockets.
l. The ˈdog's ˈmaster ˈlocked it in the ˌbarn.
m. Of ˈcourse it's ˈdark inside a ˈlocked ˌboxroom.
n. She ˈsobbed when her ˈfoster ˈfather ˈbeat her ˌharshly.
o. I've got a ˈbar of ˈchocolate in my ˌpocket.

13. / ɒ / — { Indian English / oː /
British R.P. / əʊ /

/ ɒ /	Indian English /oː/ British R.P. / əʊ /
a. cot	coat
b. dot	dote
c. cost	coast
d. tossed	toast
e. got	goat
f. rot	wrote
g. bond	boned
h. ˈtoddy	ˈtoady
i. ˈblotted	ˈbloated
j. ˈknotted	ˈnoted

k. You've ˈgot to ˈcopy these ˌnotes.
l. There's ˈnothing to ˈknow about ˌghosts.
m. ˈFollow the most ˈlightly ˈloaded ˌlorry.
n. ˈDon't talk ˈrot on the ˌtelephone.
o. I ˈwrote a ˌnote, / not a ˌnovel.
p. He ˈgroaned as I ˈtightened his ˌbonds.
q. The ˈgoat ˈtossed my ˈcoat over its ˌshoulders.
r. The ˈboat ˈsank ˈforty ˈmiles ˈoff the ˌcoast.

14. /ʊ/ — /uː/

/ʊ/	/uː/
a. pull	pool
b. full	fool
c. could	cooed
d. would	wooed
e. should	shooed

f. It's a ˈputrid ˌbook!
g. The ˈpool's ˈfuller than ˌusual.
h. ˈGo on ˈfoot through the ˌwoods.
i. Should we ˈuse a ˈwooden ˌruler?
j. The ˈwoman ˈswooned on the ˌcushions.
k. ˈWhy wouldn't you ˈuse the ˌglue?
l. They imˈpaled the ˈruler on a ˌhook.
m. We underˈstood the ˈcrew were unˈusually ˌrude.
n. A ˈmoody ˈbeauty with a ˈfull ˌfigure!
o. We'll ˈpush you in the ˈbushes, you ˌfool.

Some Assamese, Bengali, Gujarati, Bihari Hindi, Marathi and Odiya speakers have difficulty with this contrast.

15. /aɪ/ }
    /aɪ/ } — /ɔɪ/

	/ɔɪ/
a. buy	boy
b. tie	toy
c. tile	toil
d. bile	boil
e. file	foil
f. lines	loins
g. I'll	oil
h. vice	voice

i. The ˈboys are ˌrivals.

j. I'm a'fraid I've 'several ˌvices.
k. Those 'toys are 'badly deˌsigned.
l. The ˈVice-ˈPresident's 'lost his ˌvoice.
m. It's 'quite a 'simple ˌgame.
n. It's 'time to 'boil the ˌrice.
o. Our 'guide aˈvoided the ˌroughest ˌground.
p. You must 'oil it 'twice a ˌyear.
q. I'll 'buy a 'tie for my emˌployer.
r. It 'wasn't ˈnice / to 'spoil my ˌlife.

16. / ɪə / — { Indian English / eə /
             { British R.P. / ɛə /

/ ɪə /		Indian English / eə / R.P. / ɛə /
a.	here	hair
b.	fear	fair
c.	dear	dare
d.	beer	bare
e.	rear	rare
f.	peer	pare
g.	steer	stare
h.	mere	mare
i.	tear (from the eyes)	tear(rip)

j. Be ˈcareful, my ˌdear.
k. There's a 'fair 'here next ˌweek.
l. The 'mare 'reared up in ˌfright.
m. Beˈware of her ˈtears; / they're 'not ˌreal.
n. ˈWhat's the 'fare from 'here to ˌthere?
o. The ˇrarer they ˌare, / the 'dearer they ˌget.
p. The 'man in that 'chair is 'always ˌcheerful.
q. How ˈdare you ˈleer at me like ˌthat?
r. He 'flares up at the 'merest, 'barest 'hint of ˌcriticism.
s. We 'saw ˌnothing / 'stare and 'peer and ˌglare as we ˌdid.

11. Consonants

Words and sentences for practising English consonants

Plosives

1. / p / (See Section 6.2.1)

	Initial		Medial		Final
a.	poise	f.	spring	k.	trap
b.	poor	g. ap'pear		l.	rope
c.	plough	h. ru'pee		m.	lip
d.	proud	i.	'April	n.	reap
e.	'paddy	j.	'wrapping	o.	drop

- p. Does 'Prem 'still 'keep ˌpoultry?
- q. 'Prabhu's 'proud of his proˌfession.
- r. We ex'port 'pepper and ˌspices.
- s. We've 'picked a 'heap of ˌpeaches.
- t. 'English has prepoˌsitions / but 'notˌpostpoˌsitions
- u. The 'paint sprayer's 'spraying 'pink 'paint toˌday.
- v. 'Keep po'sition as you 'pass through the ˌopening.
- w. Your 'lip po'sitions are 'partly res'ponsible for your 'poor pronunciˌation.
- x. The 'fields are so 'parched it's im'possible to ˌplough them.
- y. The ˌpresent / ˌpresent ˌperfect, / ˌpreterite / and ˋpast ˌperfect / are 'some of the 'tenses of ˌEnglish.

2. / b / (See Section 6.2.1)

	Initial		Medial		Final
a.	bath	f.	ˈable	k.	hub
b.	buy	g.	aˈbout	l.	tribe
c.	brave	h.	ˈgrumble	m.	job
d.	blow	i.	ˈcupboard	n.	fib
e.	ˈbogie	j.	ˈglibness	o.	crab

p. Our ˈlabourers preˈfer ˌbaked ˌbread.
q. You ˈmisbeˈhaved beˈhind my ˌback.
r. There are ˈbeautiful ˈbuildings in Baˌnaras.
s. Would you ˈbring me that ˈbig ˌbox?
t. You can ˈbuy ˈbangles in the baˌzaar.
u. ˈBuy me a ˈbottle of ˈblue-black ˌink.
v. ˈMembers of this ˈclub are obˈliged to oˈbey the ˌrules.
w. The ˈboats were ˈblown ˈback to ˈharbour by the ˌbreeze.
x. They ˈstabbed him in the ˌback / and ˈbeat up his ˌbrother.
y. When you've ˈbought the ˌbook / I'll be ˈable to ˌborrow it.

3. /t/ (See Section 6.2.3)

	Initial		Medial		Final
a.	time	f.	ˈtatters	k.	cat
b.	tense	g.	atˈtack	l.	heat
c.	tray	h.	atˈtract	m.	beast
d.	trick	i.	ˈbattle	n.	kicked
e.	torˈmented	j.	ˈhaunted	o.	first

p. The ˈfort's ˈsaid to be ˌhaunted.
q. ˈTry to ˈtouch the ˈtiger's ˌtail.
r. ˈPut it in the ˋpast ˌtense.

s. It ˈisnˈt quite ˈtime to ˈgo to ˌtown.
t. ˈHitting below the ˈbelt is a ˋdirty ˌtrick.
u. Itˈs the ˈfirst ˈtime weˈve atˈtacked by ˌnight.
v. ˈToddy-tappers colˈlect ˈjuice from the ˈtops of ˌtrees.
w. Siˈalkot was one of the ˈgreatest ˈtank ˈbattles in ˌhistory.
x. He ˈshot the ˈcheetah unˇsportingly / from the ˈtop of a ˌtruck.
y. At ˈthis time of the ˌyear / it gets ˈhot at ˈhalf past ˌten.

4. / d / (See Section 6.2.3)

	Initial		Medial		Final
a.	dark	f.	ˈtrader	k.	hard
b.	dry	g.	ˈbadly	l.	sad
c.	drip	h.	ˈsaddle	m.	breed
d.	ˈdealer	i.	ˈaddled	n.	dried
e.	deˈsire	j.	adˈdition	o.	pleased

p. Theyˈd ˈhad a ˈbad ˌday.
q. ˈWild ˈdogs deˈvoured the ˌbody.
r. Add aˈnother ˈhundred and ˈfifty ˌpounds.
s. ˈDrought ˈdried up the ˋpaddy ˌfields.
t. Itˈs ˈmade of ˈdrip-ˋdry ˌfabric.
u. Weˈd ˈeaten ˈdry ˈdal for ˈtwo ˌdays.
v. ˈBasic eduˈcation is unˈdoubtedly ˋwidespread in ˌIndia.
w. Do you ˈknow the ˈdate of Indeˌpendence ˌDay?
x. The daˈcoits were ˌrounded up / and their ˈplunder ˈredisˌtributed.
y. It was a ˋbad ˌplay / but it had a draˈmatic ˌending.

5. / k / (See Section 6.2.4)

	Initial		Medial		Final
a.	choir	f.	ˈdarkness	k.	ache
b.	clear	g.	ˈbreakage	l.	teak
c.	cry	h.	ˈbackground	m.	lake
d.	queue	i.	obsˈcure	n.	sick
e.	ˈcurry	j.	ˈankle	o.	bark

p. ˈRock ˈoutcrops ocˈcur ˋfrequently in the ˌDeccan.
q. The ˈfactory's ˈclosed becˈause of the ˌstrike.
r. I ˈcouldn't ˈcome to ˌcollege / beˈcause I'd ˈcaught a ˌcold.
s. You ˈmake it from a ˈkind of ˈclotted ˌcream.
t. You ˈcan't keep ˈliquids in that ˌbucket / because it ˌleaks.
u. I ˈcouldn't ˈcount the ˋcrowd at the ˌhockey ˌcup ˌfinal.
v. ˈWhen you ˌspeak, / speak ˈquietly and ˌconfidently / and you'll conˌvince them.
w. ˈCauliflowers, ˈcabbages and ˌleeks, / cost ˋmore in the ˌmarket this ˌweek.
x. The ˈback ran aˌcross, / ˌtackled, / and made a ˈquick ˈkick up the ˌfield.
y. When he was ˈknocked ˌdown, / he ˈbroke his ˈankle and ˈcracked his ˌskull.

6. / g / (See Section 6.2.4)

	Initial		Medial		Final
a.	gun	f.	ˈbeggar	k.	dog
b.	goal	g.	ˈargue	l.	big
c.	ground	h.	ˈpregnant	m.	sag
d.	glow	i.	ˈwriggle	n.	plague
e.	ˈgladden	j.	exˈist	o.	rogue

p. Please forˈgive my ˈgroundless ˌgrumbling.
q. I igˈnored my ˈyounger ˈsister's ˈeager ˌgiggling.

Consonants

r. ˈGo and get your ˈgun and your ˌdog.
s. In ˈAugust there was a ˈplague of giˈgantic ˌgrasshoppers.
t. I was exˈhausted by the ˈgreat ˈgusts of ˌwind.
u. We've ˈgot to get to ˈAgra to ˈgreet our ˌguests.
v. We've ˈgot to ˈguard the ˇgold in the ˌwaggons / against ˌgangsters.
w. He'll be ˈglad to get a ˈgood ˈbook as a ˌgift.
x. The ˈgrass grows ˋtall in the ˌjungle / and the ˌground's ˌrugged.
y. The ˈbigger of the ˈrobbers ˌgrabbed me / and ˈthreatened me with a ˌdagger.

Affricates

7. / tʃ / (See Section 6.3)

	Initial		Medial		Final
a.	choose	f.	ˈmatched	k.	bench
b.	child	g.	ˈarchery	l.	march
c.	cheese	h.	ˈfeature	m.	peach
d.	chair	i.	ˈreaching	n.	wretch
e.	ˈcharming	j.	ˈriches	o.	reˈsearch

p. I ˈwatched him ˈteaching ˌchildren.
q. That ˈchap's ˈcheerful by ˌnature.
r. Our aˈchievements in ˈspeech are ˌmatchless!
s. I ˈchose ˈChina for my poˈlitical reˌsearch.
t. The ˈwretched ˈwatchman ˈdidn't ˈcatch the ˌthief!
u. ˈFetch a ˈchair from the desˌpatch-ˌoffice.
v. My ˈwatch ˈisn't a ˈpatch on ˌCharles's.
w. I ˈdon't find ˈchess such a beˈwitching ˌgame.
x. He's ˈsearching for a ˌwife / who's 'charming as well as ˌrich.

y. He had indiˇgestion / after ˈeating ˈchicken ˌcurry, / ˌchops, / / ˌchips / and ˌcheese for his ˌsupper.

8. / dʒ / (See Section 6.3)

	Initial		Medial		Final
a.	June	f.	ˈmargin	k.	gorge
b.	jam	g.	ˈlargely	l.	bridge
c.	giant	h.	ˈfrigid	m.	huge
d.	jewel	i.	ˈtragedy	n.	reˈvenge
e.	ˈgentle	j.	reˈfrigerator	o.	ˈorange

p. ˈOrange pyˈjamas ˈaren't genˌteel.
q. We're obˈliged to adˈjust the arˌrangements.
r. I'm a geˈologist, / ˈnot a geˌographer.
s. The Regiˈmental ˈSergeant ˈMajor is a ˌsavage.
t. There's a ˈlarge ˈlog-ˈjam in the ˌgorge.
u. ˈGeorge is going to ˈjudge the ˈjazz compeˌtition.
v. I ˈjoined ˌages aˌgo. / ˈThree ˈyears last ˌJanuary.
w. The ˈtragedy had a ˈstrange efˈfect on his ˌjudgement.
x. We ˌput a ˈhuge ˈcharge of ˈgelignite ˈunder the ˌbridge.
y. ˈJim's got a ˈsmudge on the ˈbridge of his ˌnose.

Fricatives

9. / f / (See Section 6.4.1)

	Initial		Medial		Final
a.	fold	f.	graft	k.	half
b.	fear	g.	ˈlaughing	l.	brief
c.	field	h.	afˈfair	m.	safe
d.	ˈphantom	i.	aˈfraid	n.	cough
e.	fanˈtastic	j.	ˈafterwards	o.	rough

Consonants

p. Fe|roze's |cough sounds |awfully ˌrough.
q. Your |fish isn't ˌfresh eˌnough.
r. It's |awful how ˌstiff Iˌ feel.
s. We've e|nough |food to |feed ˌforty.
t. His |flat |feet make him ˌshuffle.
u. I've a |photograph of |Freddy looking ˌfurious.
v. We went |further ˌup / and |got |half-ˌfrozen.
w. I'd pre|fer only |half a ˈpound of ˌcoffee.
x. I |fear it's ˈfutile to ˌteach me phoˌnetics.
y. I'm aˈfraid it's |all a ˌfarce, / but |fill up these |four ˌforms.

10. /v/ (See Section 6.4.1)

	Initial		Medial		Final
a.	vile	f.	|river	k.	save
b.	view	g.	|weaver	l.	grieve
c.	|vowel	h.	re|veal	m.	love
d.	ve|randa	i.	de|voted	n.	move
e.	va|cation	j.	be|haviour	o.	a|live

p. We've |voted him |vice-ˌpresident.
q. My |novel was |vilely reˌviewed.
r. The |Russel's |viper is |very ˌvenomous.
s. We've |saved |five |vases from the ˌshop.
t. Have you |seen the |view from my veˌranda?
u. I |live in a |village above the ˌvalley.
v. I |vowed |never to |fall in ˌlove aˌgain.
w. We've |priced that |carving at |seventy |five ruˌpees.
x. The |voyage |ends at ˌVenice / and |then we have to |fly to Viˌenna.
y. In |view of |all the |evidence of your |vicious beˌhaviour / we |have to ˌpunish you.

11. / θ / (See Section 6.4.2)

	Initial		Medial		Final
a.	thick	f.	fifths	k.	path
b.	thought	g.	ˈbirthday	l.	both
c.	thanks	h.	ˈtoothless	m.	mouth
d.	thrive	i.	ˈpanther	n.	wrath
e.	through	j.	ˈfaithful	o.	dearth

p. Toˈmorrow's my ˈthirty-ˈthird ˌbirthday.
q. The ˈpanther's ˈold and ˌtoothless.
r. My ˈhead's ˌthrobbing / and my ˌteeth ˌhurt.
s. The ˈrock's ˈjust beneath the ˌearth ˌhere.
t. They're ˈtoo ˈthin to be ˈreally ˌhealthy.
u. I ˈdon't think the ˈcloth's ˌworth it.
v. ˈThree ˈfourths and ˈone ˈeighth make ˈseven ˌeighths.
w. I've auˈthority to ˈthank you for your ˌthoroughness.
x. ˈBoth the ˈfirst and the ˈfourth ˌthefts / were comˈmitted by ˌday.
y. There were ˈthick ˈthorn ˌbushes / along the ˈpath through the ˌforest.

12. / ð / (See Section 6.4.2)

	Initial		Medial		Final
a.	this	f.	ˈwreathed	k.	bathe
b.	though	g.	ˈbreathing	l.	seethe
c.	them	h.	wiˈthout	m.	smooth
d.	there	i.	ˈeither	n.	scythe
e.	that	j.	ˈmother	o.	with

p. They ˈloathe their ˌmother-in-law.
q. ˈLeather ˈshoes go ˌfarther.
r. He was ˈseething with ˌrage.
s. My ˈfather ˈisn't with them, / ˌthough.
t. He ˈscythed ˈsmoothly through the ˌgrass.

u. The ˈtall oneˈs my ˈother ˌbrother.
v. Iˈd ˌrather ˈyou went ˌthere ˌthis time.
w. ˈThat boy can ˈstand on his ˈhead without ˌbreathing.
x. ˈEither theyˈll oˈbey the ˌrules / or they ˈwonˈt ˌbathe.
y. Weˈve ˈfed them and ˈclothed them without ofˈficial ˌbacking.

13. /s/ (Section 6.4.3)

	Initial		Medial		Final
a.	same	f.	fast	k.	pass
b.	speak	g.	exˈtend	l.	rice
c.	screw	h.	beˈseech	m.	waits
d.	strike	i.	conˈceal	n.	caps
e.	ˈceiling	j.	poˈtassium	o.	reˈlease

p. ˈSaccharine ˈtastes ˈsweeter than ˌsugar.
q. ˈSteam esˈcapes from the ˌspout.
r. ˈPut some ˈsalt in the ˌstew.
s. The ˈstudents seem to ˈwant an exˌtension.
t. It would be ˈstupid to ˈdrink poˈtassium ˌcyanide.
u. ˈDonˈt ˈspeak ˌswiftly / ˈsay it ˈslightly more ˌslowly.
v. The ˈschoolmaster seemed ˈsad / when we supˈported the ˌstrike.
w. Itˈs ˈuseless to ˈsay you ˈdidnˈt ˈsteal the ˌsuitcase.
x. The ˈtrain ˈwhistled as it ˈstood at the ˈlevel ˌcrossing.
y. Thereˈs a ˈregistered ˈparcel for ˈSita at the ˌpost office.

14. / z / (See Section 6.4.3)

	Initial		Medial		Final
a.	zeal	f.	deˈsire	k.	lose
b.	zoo	g.	ˈbusiness	l.	hours
c.	zinc	h.	exˈhaust	m.	hives

d. ˈzero i. ˈreason n. ˈbirds
e. ˈzenith j. baˈzaar
o. The ˈbees ˈbuzzed round the ˌhives.
p. The baˈzaar's ˈclosed on ˌFeast ˈDays.
q. Her ˈgarden's got ˈdozens of ˌroses.
r. The ˈzoo's easily ˈfive ˎmiles from ˌhere.
s. The ˈbreezes ˈblew the ˈleaves from the ˌtrees.
t. The ˈgirl's ˈarms were a ˈmass of ˌbruises.
u. It ˈbaffles me how ˈlizards exˈist in the ˌdesert.
v. As ˈwell as being ˌzealous / he ˈuses his ˌbrains.
w. There ˈisn't enough ˎgrazing in the ˌfields for the ˌanimals.
x. It was aˇmazing / that Aleˈxander got as ˈfar as the ˈborders of ˌIndia.

15. / ʃ / (See Section 6.4.4)

	Initial		Medial		Final
a.	sheep	f.	ˈfashion	k.	trash
b.	shore	g.	ˈfission	l.	fish
c.	sure	h.	ˈportion	m.	marsh
d.	shrew	i.	ˈanxious	n.	ˈpolish
e.	shriek	j.	ˈashes	o.	mousˈtache

p. ˈRacial segreˈgation is obˌnoxious.
q. ˈShashi ˈshaved off his mousˌtache.
r. ˈSheela's amˌbitious / but ˈrather ˌrash.
s. Are you ˈsure you ˈsheared ˌall the ˌsheep?
t. We've ofˈficial ˈsanction for your ˈtrip to ˈShanti Niˌketan.
u. ˈGo and ˈwash my ˌshirts / and ˈbrush my ˌshoes.
v. She's ˈhad her ˈshare of ˈsugar from the ˌration ˌshop.
w. Our ˈmission at the Uˈnited ˈNations is to enˈsure ˌpeace.
x. ˈDrive ˌcautiously / and you'll ˈget a reˈmission on your inˌsurance.

y. The 'wind's‚freshening / so the 'fishermen will 'have to re'turn to ˎshore.

16. / ʒ / (See Section 6.4.4)

	Medial		Final
a.	'leisure	g.	rouge
b.	'treasure	h.	beige
c.	'pleasure	i.	'barrage
d.	e'rosion	j.	'mirage
e.	di'vision		

k. 'Measure the de'gree of corˎrosion.
l. The di'vision of the 'treasure was 'not ‚easy.
m. We were 'shocked by the dis'closure of the ˎH-bomb exˌplosion.
n. The 'seizure of the 'treasure was ˎmy deˌcision.
o. The 'number of 'casualties in the in'vasion was imˎmeasurable.
p. We need 'barrages on the 'river against ˎsoil eˌrosion.
q. There'll be di'vision of 'labour after the tranˎsitional ˌperiod.
r. That per'formance of *Measure for Measure* was a ˎreal ˌpleasure.
s. 'Mirages are the 'usual il'lusions of the ˎdesert.
t. I 'don't know 'why he 'painted his ˌgarage / 'beige and ˎbronze.

17. / h / (See Section 6.4.5)

	Initial		Medial
a.	hot	f.	'cowherd
b.	hear	g.	'racehorse
c.	half	h.	be'hind
d.	hu'manity	i.	per'haps

e. who   j. Bi'har

Note: No / h / sound in
- k. 'honest
- l. hour
- m. heir
- n. 'honour
- o. 'Hari's 'hardly ˌhuman.
- p. His 'racehorse was 'left be ˌhind.
- q. 'Who'll 'help me 'build my ˌhouse?
- r. The 'whole 'village was 'hoarding ˌgrain.
- s. 'Whose 'hat is 'that in the ˌhall?
- t. It 'might be hisᵛtoric / but it's 'unhyˌgienic.
- u. I 'hear it's 'hot and 'humid in Maˌdras.
- v. Hari'dwar is a 'holy 'town on the ˌGanga.
- w. He's 'going on a 'tiger 'hunt in Biˌhar.
- x. Per'haps I'll 'have some 'news in 'half an ˌhour.

Nasals

18. / m / (See Section 6.5.1)

	Initial		Medial		Final
a.	mile	f.	'bombed	k.	same
b.	mixed	g.	'harmful	l.	team
c.	'mostly	h.	'formless	m.	spasm
d.	'mother	i.	'temple	n.	atom
e.	ma'laria	j.	'dimly	o.	'communism

- p. We 'measure by the ˎmetric ˌsystem.
- q. Are there 'many u'ranium 'mines in ˌIndia?
- r. 'Ram 'isn't a ˎcalm ˌman, / he's 'most temperaˌmental.
- s. 'Most of us 'met them in the ˎpark.
- t. Do 'Tamilnadu and Ma'dras 'mean the 'same ˌthing?

u. We must ˈknow the ˈmaximum and ˈminimum ˌtemperatures.
v. She is the ˈleader of a ˈwomen's ˌmovement.
w. ˈMust you ˈkeep your ˈtame ˈmice in my ˌbedroom?
x. ˈAssam is a ˈland of ˈmountains, ˈstreams and maˈjestic ˌrivers.
y. ˈMummy went for a ˈholiday in the ˈmountains last ˌmonth.

19. / n / (See Section 6.5.2)

	Initial		Medial		Final
a.	nuts	f.	tent	k.	earn
b.	nice	g.	bend	l.	sign
c.	near	h.	deˈny	m.	brown
d.	knife	i.	enˈsure	n.	beˈgin
e.	knock	j.	enˈnoble	o.	ˈmotion

p. ˈTen ˈnines are ˌninety.
q. ˈNandita ˈdoesn't ˈearn enough ˌmoney.
r. I ˈdon't ˈmind the ˌnoise.
s. There are ˈnone ˈnearer at ˌhand.
t. He's ˈdefinitely ˈnot a ˈnice ˌperson.
u. The monˈsoon ˈrains beˈgin in ˌJune.
v. ˈSen doesn't underˈstand the fiˈnancial negotiˌations.
w. They ˈdon't know ˈnearly enough ˌHindi.
x. Have you ˈseen my ˈnotes on ˈNatya ˌShastra?
y. He's the ˈnew ˈMinister for ˈMines in the ˌCabinet.

20. / ŋ / (See Section 6.5.3)

	Medial		Final
a.	trunk	f.	bring
b.	ˈsinger	g.	rung
c.	ˈuncle	h.	ˈsinging
d.	ˈjungle	i.	ˈlonging

e. ˈtriangle   j. aˈmong
k. The ˈcar ˈsprings are ˌcreaking.
l. The ˈclanging of the ˈtemple ˌgongs.
m. There's ˈsomething ˈwrong with my ˌankle.
n. The ˈtiger's the ˈking of the ˌjungle.
o. They ˈthronged to ˈlisten to ˈSubbulakshmi's ˌsinging.
p. There's ˈno ˈdrinking ˈwater in the ˌtanks.
q. I'm ˈlonging to ˈsee my ˈuncle next ˌspring.
r. I fell ˈoff the ˈtop ˌrung / and ˈsprained my ˌankle.
s. You ˈneed a ˈlong ˈstring to ˈhang it ˌup with.
t. He ˈflung out of the ˈroom and ˈbanged the ˌdoor.

Lateral

21. / l / (See Section 6.6)

	Initial		Medial		Final
a.	lead	f.	split	k.	ball
b.	lame	g.	flame	l.	feel
c.	last	h.	ˈfeelings	m.	ˈbottle
d.	lock	i.	ˈpillar	n.	ˈmuddle
e.	liar	j.	aˈlive	o.	ˈcripple

p. ˈGelignite exˈplodes ˌloudly.
q. I'll inˈsult the ˌblackguard!
r. ˈBalu fell ˈoff the ˌladder.
s. It'll be imˈpossible to ˌleave now.
t. The ˈpeasant ˈfeels that ˈcattle are ˌwealth.
u. ˈWhen shall we ˈleave for the ˌNilgiris?
v. ˈBlow the ˈflames ˈsoftly till they ˈleap ˌup.
w. The ˈPost Office deˈlivers ˈmillions of ˈletters and ˌparcels.
x. ˈMorals are ˈsaid to be ˈmore than ˈusually ˌlax now.

y. The ˈrebels dealt ˈvilely with ˈall they called ˈbloated ˌcapitalists.

Frictionless continuant

22. / r / (See Section 6.7)

	Initial		Medial		Final (in Indian English)
a.	rough	f.	shrine	k.	four
b.	round	g.	front	l.	fear
c.	rock	h.	ˈbarrel	m.	stare
d.	write	i.	ˈtragic	n.	ˈwater
e.	wrap	j.	scream	o.	ˈbetter

p. She ˈtried to ˈscream ˌshrilly.
q. Your ˈface is growing ˈredder and ˌredder.
r. ˈAll the ˈthree ˈrobbers have been arˌrested.
s. ˈRavi's arˈranged for ˈthree ˈsecond-class ˌsleeping ˌberths.
t. We ˈtried to reˈmain ˋneutral in the ˌstruggle.
u. ˈIf I'm ˌright / there's a ˋcross-roads around ˌhere.
v. ˈAre there ˈcoral ˈreefs ˈoff the ˈshores of ˌKerala?
w. There's a ˈreason for our reˈmaining in the ˌcountry.
x. The ˈtrack through the ˈforest's ˈvery ˈdangerous after ˌdark.
y. ˈGo through the ˌtrees / and you'll ˈfind the ˈferry across the ˌriver.

Semi-Vowels

23. /j/ (See Section 6.8.1)

	Initial		Medial
a.	ewe	f.	view
b.	your	g.	huge
c.	yell	h.	'beauty
d.	'yearly	i.	'pupil
e.	'usual	j.	ex'cuses

k. You 'yawned ˌhugely.
l. I ac'cuse you of ˌusury.
n. The 'Union 'met as 'usual ˌyesterday.
o. 'Years a'go she was a ˌbeauty.
p. We'll 'carry ammu'nition on ˌmule back.
q. You've got a ˋlurid* ˌsense of ˌhumour.
r. There was a 'queue at the 'bureau on ˌTuesday.
s. 'What's the 'future for the 'spice 'trade with ˌEurope?
t. He's the most' useless 'human 'being I've 'met in ˌyears.
u. You can get a 'good 'view of the ˌyachts / from over ˌyonder.

25. / w / (See Section 6.8.2)

	Initial		Medial
a.	waste	f.	switch
b.	which	g.	squeeze
c.	white	h.	'always
d.	well	i.	re'ward
e.	one	j.	'dwelling

---

*lurid can be pronounced either as / 'ljuərɪd / or as / 'luərɪd /.

k. ˈWhisper it ˌquietly.
l. Were they ˈwilling to ˌwait?
m. Those ˈwomen are ˈwonderful ˌweavers.
n. ˈWouldn't you ˈwant to ˈwork ˌwell?
o. I ˈwish to ˈgo for a ˌwalk.
p. Would you ˈlike to ˈwork on the ˌrailways?
q. I ˈwarned you she had a ˈwicked ˌsquint.
r. A ˈwheel fell ˈoff ˈsomewhere along the ˌway.
s. I ˈwon't ˈwear a ˈwhite ˈsari at the ˌwedding.
t. The ˈwestern ˈslopes of the ˈWestern ˈGhats are ˈwell ˌwooded.

Practice in consonant contrasts

1. /p/ —/f/

	/p/ [ph]	/f/
a.	pan	fan
b.	paint	faint
c.	peer	fear
d.	past	fast
e.	prayed	frayed
f.	pail	fail
g.	port	fort
h.	pig	fig
i.	pull	full
j.	pyre	fire

k. Artiˈficial ˈfibres are perˈhaps ˌcheaper.
l. ˈFlames flared ˈup from the ˈfuneral ˌpyre.
m. The ˈpriests ˈprayed for a ˈfull ˌhour.
n. ˈIs there eˈnough ˈpaint for the paˌvilion?
o. It apˈpears there's a ˈfootpath to the ˌfort.
p. The poˈlice inˈspector ˈfound out aˈbout the ˌforgeries.
q. ˈPrem pulled ˈpails of ˈfresh ˈwater from the ˌwell.

r. She ˈfelt ˈfaint when she ˈpeered over the ˌcliffs.
s. It's ˈfar ˈpast the ˈtime for the ˈferry to ˌclose.
t. The ˈprawns fell ˈout of the ˈfrying ˈpan into the ˌfire.

Some Indian speakers have difficulty with this contrast.

2. /b/—/v/

	/b/	/v/
a.	best	vest
b.	bile	vile
c.	bent	vent
d.	bat	vat
e.	bale	veil
f.	ban	van
g.	beer	veer
h.	bet	vet
i.	boat	vote
j.	ˈberry	ˈvery

k. ˈRavi broke ˈfive ˈbig ˌvases.
l. The ˈnew ˈbaby's ˈvery ˈvery ˌsmall.
m. Even the ˈbest ˈbeer tastes ˌvile.
n. ˈRavi sleeps ˈbest on the veˌranda.
o. Have you ˈbeen to ˈVed's beˌfore?
p. I've ˈlived in Benˈgal since ˌboyhood.
q. Does the ˈriver ever ˈburst its ˌbanks?
r. The ˈbiggest ˈvillages are aˈbove the ˋriver ˌvalley.
s. Mr. ˈVeeraswami ˈvoted for ˈBalaᵛsundaram/as the ˋbest ˌcandidate.
t. The ˈvet arˈrived by ˈboat because the ˈbridge ˌbroke.

Some Assamese, Bengali, Hindi and Odiya speakers have difficulty with this contrast.

3. / t / —/ θ /

	/t/	/ θ /
a.	tin	thin
b.	tie	thigh
c.	tank	thank
d.	taught	thought
e.	trill	thrill
f.	boat	both
g.	rot	wrath
h.	debt	death
i.	welt	wealth
j.	dirt	dearth

k. ˈDeath ˈcomes at ˈlast to ˌall.
l. ˈBoth ˈboats' ˈthwarts were ˈstaved ˌin.
m. ˈStir it ˈthoroughly till it ˌthickens.
n. It was a ˈrotten ˈthing to ˌhappen.
o. He ˈdoesn't have to ˈthank you for ˌanything.
p. Your ˈgift was ˈnot much ˈbetter than ˌnothing.
q. The ˈtimbers were ˈriddled ˈthrough and ˈthrough with ˌtermites.
r. The ˈtheme of my ˈlast ˈtalk is ˈcitizens' ˌrights.
s. What a ˈthrill to ˈcatch the ˈthief so ˌeasily.
t. I ˈdidn't ˈthink we had ˈsuch a ˈthin ˈtime at ˌOoty.

4. / d / —/ ð /

	/d/	/ð/
a.	den	then
b.	dine	thine
c.	dough	though
d.	suede	swathe
e.	load	loathe
f.	laid	lathe

g. ˈdither ˈthither
h. ˈudder ˈother
i. ˈbladder ˈblather
j. ˈbreeding ˈbreathing
k. ˈBreathe ˌhard.
l. The ˈother ˈudder's ˈbadly inˌfected.
m. He's a ˈskilled ˈ\lathe ˌoperator.
n. I ˈcouldn't find the ˈother ˌdoor.
o. I ˈ\loathe the ˌdesert. /Don't ˌyou?
p. ˈDidn't you ˈdo it ˌthat time, then?
q. They ˈeach ˈcarried a ˈbundle of ˌclothes.
r. The ˈriver's ˈcrowded with ˈbathers at the ˌSangam
s. There's a ˈvery ˈodd ˈold ˈ\woman ˌdown that ˌalley.
t. The maˈchine ˈcut a ˈbroad ˈ\swathe / down the ˈmiddle of the ˌfield.

5. / tʃ / — / s /

/ tʃ /	/ s /
a. chips	sips
b. church	search
c. chill	sill
d. cheer	sear

e. ˈPeople in Maˈdras like ˈsambar and ˌchillies.
f. We ˈsaw the ˈchildren ˌyesterday.
g. The ˈchickens ˈscratched aˈround outˌside.
h. I ˈcaught a ˈchill last Deˌcember.
i. ˈSita ˈwatched the ˈmatch for ˈseven ˌminutes.
j. The ˈmatches ˈfell all ˈover the ˌmats.
k. The triˈumphal ˈarch colˈlapsed on the proˌcession.
l. There were ˈsix ˈregiments in the ˌmarch past.
m. The ˈchampionship ˈchess ˈmatches ˈtake place at ˌSiliguri.

n. The ˈcoach ˈstuck in ˌmelted ˎpitch on the ˌroad.

Some Assamese speakers have difficulty with this contrast.

6. / dʒ / — / z /

	/ d ʒ /	/ z /
a.	jest	zest
b.	Jew	zoo
c.	budge	buzz
d.	gauge	gaze
e.	wage	ways
f.	rage	raise
g.	change	chains
h.	barge	bars
i.	ˈjealous	ˈzealous
j.	ˈregion	ˈreason

k. ˈZebras ˈdon't like ˎcages.
l. There's a ˈfreeze on ˎwage inˌcreases.
m. The ˈtown's justˎbuzzing with ˌrumours.
n. He's got ˈno ˈreason to be ˎjealous.
o. Mr ˈGeorge says he ˈcomes from ˎKerala.
p. A ˈnarrow-gauge ˈrailway runs ˈup to the reˎsort.
q. He's ˈworked for an ˈadvertising ˈagency since Juˎly.
r. If the asˈtrologer aˎgrees / the ˈmarriage is in ˎJanuary.
s. There are ˈno ˈchanges in our ˈplans for ˈregional deˎvelopment.
t. The engiˈneers found ˈways to sling ˎchains across the ˌgorges.

Some Hindi and Odiya speakers have difficulty with this contrast.

7. / dʒ / — / ʒ /

	/ dʒ /	/ ʒ /
a.	ˈledger	ˈleisure
b.	ˈlegion	ˈlesion

c. The ˈsurgeon made a ˈlarge in ˌcision.
d. The ˈjudge's deˈcision desˈtroyed our ilˌlusions.
e. ˈSoil eˈrosion's ˈnot just a ˌjoke.
f. We're ˈnot obˈliged to beˈlieve in ˌvisions.
g. It was a ˈstrange but ˈpleasurable ocˌcasion.
h. There was a ˈhuge exˈplosion under the ˌbridge.
i. The jaˈwans ˈpledged themselves to ˈhalt the in ˌvasion.
j. The poˈlice deˈmanded the ˈseizure of the ˌledgers.
k. There's a diˈvision between the geoᵛgraphical / and the geoˈlogical aspects.
l. Our ˈparents' deˈcision was for a ˈmarriage in ˌJune.

Some Indian speakers have difficulty with this contrast.

8. / v / — / w /

	/ v /	/ w /
a.	vie	why
b.	vend	wend
c.	veal	wheel
d.	vest	west
e.	vine	wine
f.	verse	worse
g.	vile	while
h.	veil	wail
i.	vein	wane
j.	vim	whim

k. We've ˈvowed to ˌwin.

Consonants

l. The ˈweather's ˈvile this ˌweek.
m. ˈWhat will ˈnext ˌyear reˌveal?
n. We'll ˈvisit you ˈtwice a ˌweek.
o. My ˈverse gets ˈworse and ˌworse.
p. ˈWear a ˈwarm ˈvest in ˌwinter.
q. She's a ˈwoman of ˈvicious ˌwhims.
r. They've ˈworn ˈveils for ˈquite a ˌwhile.
s. ˈOnce you ˈplayed the ˈveena ˈvery ˌwell.
t. My ˈveins have the ˈwine of ˌyouth in them.

Most Indian speakers have difficulty with this contrast.

9. / s / — / z /

	/ s /	/ z /
a.	seal	zeal
b.	sink	zinc
c.	dose	doze
d.	mace	maze
e.	loose	lose
f.	peace	peas
g.	rice	rise
h.	fleece	fleas
i.	niece	knees
j.	bass (in music)	bays

k. They reˈcited some ˈprayers to Saˈraswati.
l. It's an ˈalloy with a ˈzinc ˌbase.
m. ˈRises in ˈrice ˈprices must be ˌstopped.
n. My ˈnieces were ˈpleased with their ˌpresents.
o. ˈTyphus is a diˈsease ˈcarried by ˌfleas.
p. We got ˈlost in a ˈmaze of ˌstreets.
q. My ˈknees are ˌsore/and my ˈfoot ˌhurts.
r. It's too ˈhot for ˌseals/in the ˈlocal ˌzoo.

s. He ˈscored a suˈperb ˈcentury for the ˈSouth ˌZone.
t. I ˈwon a ˈprize by ˈsolving a ˈcrossword ˈpuzzle corˌrectly.

10. / s / — / ʃ /

	/ s /	/ ʃ /
a.	sift	shift
b.	sip	ship
c.	seep	sheep
d.	seal	she'll
e.	same	shame
f.	sow (v.)	show
g.	sack	shack
h.	sea	she
i.	ass	ash
j.	mess	mesh

k. ˈClose-meshed ˈnets are most ˌnecessary
l. ˈSilken ˈsheets are a ˌluxury.
m. She'll ˈsift the ˈash ˈseven ˌtimes.
n. The ˈrice ˈration seems ˈscarcely sufˌficient.
o. ˈSita ˈshowed me her ˈsnakeskin ˌshoes.
p. ˈShankar ˈsorted ˈsea-shells on the ˌseashore.
q. ˈWhere shall we ˈshift the ˌsoil to?
r. The ˈwhole ˈnation will ˈshare the ˌsacrifices.
s. It's a ˈshame she's ˈsuch an ˌass.
t. There are ˈseventy-ˈsix ˈsheep on the ˌfarm.

Some Assamese. Bengali, Hindi and Odiya speakers have difficulty with this contrast.

11. / z / — / ʒ /

a. He's desˈerted on ˈseveral ocˌcasions.
b. His ˈsneezes reˈsulted in a ˌseizure.

c. We've ˈno ilˈlusions about his ˌzeal.
d. ˈFurther diˈvision would be a diˌsaster.
e. She's a ˈwoman of ˈzest and ˌvision.
f. He was imˈprisoned for emˈbezzlement after the disˌclosures.
g. An examiˈnation of the ˈwound shows undeˈsirable adˌhesions.
h. ˈMetal corˈrosion is ˈworst in the ˎcoastal ˌzone.
i. In the conˈfusion he ˈchanged his ˈzero into a ˌhundred.
j. ˈNaini ˈTal's a ˈgood reˌsort / for ˈall ˈkinds of ˎleisure acˌtivities.

Some Assamese, Bengali, Gujarati, Hindi, Kashmiri, Odiya and Urdu speakers have difficulty with this contrast.

12. / ʃ / — / ʒ /

      / ʃ /   / ʒ /
a. Conˈfucian conˈfusion
b. It's a ˈcomplex ˈfission-ˈfusion ˈthermoˎnuclear reˌaction.
c. The ˈtwo ˈnations are on a colˎlision ˌcourse.
d. They've got ˈqueer ˈnotions about ˈmultipliˈcation and diˌvision.
e. ˈWomen's ˈfashion ˈgives me sufˈficient ˈcause for deˌrision.
f. She's in a ˈstate of ˈshock and conˌfusion.
g. He made ˈno alˈlusion to the ˈRussian ˌspace shot.
h. The reˈport of an inˈvasion was a comˈplete ˌfiction.
i. Their ˈpleasures may be deˌlicious / but they're ˈsomewhat un ˌusual.
j. This is an ocˈcasion for ˈrationing on a ˎnational ˌbasis.

k. Your ex'clusion from 'office was a re'sult of your 'over-am ˌbition.

Some Kannada, Malâyalam, Tamil and Telugu speakers have difficulty with this contrast.

13. / r / — / l /

	/r/	/l/
a.	red	lead (metal)
b.	reef	leaf
c.	road	load
d.	reach	leech
e.	rung	lung
f.	rein	lane
g.	rid	lid
h.	write	light
i.	wrong	long
j.	'river	'liver

k. The ˇlight's ˌwrong for phoˌtography.
l. I 'wanted ˇred ˌleather/ 'not ˌyellow.
m. I've 'written my ˇlast ˌletter to ˌRenu.
n. 'Hold the 'reins in your ˇleft ˌhand.
o. I 'rowed 'quickly ac'ross the 'silent ˌlake.
p. There's a 'large 'black 'cobra 'coiled up on the veˌranda.
q. We'll 'reach Cal'cutta by 'dark if the 'train isn't ˌlate.
r. 'Ram 'loves 'strong 'hot ˌcurry / but it's 'very 'bad for his ˌliver.
s. An as'trologer will 'read your ˌfate / in the 'lines of your ˌpalm.
t. The 'Brahma'putra 'River 'rises in Tiˌbet / and 'flows 'down to the 'plains of ˌAssam.

Some Assamese speakers have difficulty with this contrast.

12. Consonant Clusters

Initial Clusters

1. /pl-/
   - a. please
   - b. plight
   - c. play
   - d. plank
   - e. plum
   - f. plain
   - g. plough
   - h. ˈplaudits
   - i. ˈplenty
   - j. ˈplaster
   - k. It's a ˈpliable ˌplastic maˌterial.
   - l. The ˈplural of ˈplace is ˌplaces.
   - m. It's ˈplain you'll ˈnever ˈplay for ˌIndia.
   - n. There are ˈplenty of ˌplums this ˌyear.
   - o. Please ˈdon't ˌleave me in this ˌplight.
   - p. He's a ˌpleasant ˌfellow, / but a ˌplodder.
   - q. The ˈstrings are ˈplucked with a ˌplectrum.
   - r. The ˈbucket of ˈplaster ˈfell off the ˌplank,
   - s. The ˈcrowd's ˈplaudits rang ˈpleasantly in his ˌears.
   - t. We must ˈplead for ˈmore ˈfunds for ˌfamily planning.

2. /pr-/
   - a. pray
   - b. prick
   - c. prod
   - d. prove
   - e. pride
   - f. prone
   - g. ˈprattle
   - h. preˈserve
   - i. They ˈpromised ˈrapid ˌprogress.

j. The ˈproˈprietor's ˈprone to exˈagge ˌration.
k. Your ˈpride will ˈprove your ˌdownfall.
l. They ˈpray ˈprostrate on the ˌground.
m. May ˈGod preˈserve me from ˈprattling ˌfools.
n. Our ˈprofits are proˈportional to our ˌefforts.
o. The ˈcompany prosˈpectus underˈlines our ˈpresent prosˌperity.
p. The ˈdoctor presˈcribed a ˈhigh ˈprotein ˌdiet.
q. The ˈprincipal will ˈsee you in ˌprivate.
r. I've ˈno obˌjection / proˈvided you proˈtect our ˌinterests.

3. /pj-/
   a. ˈpure
   b. ˈpuny
   c. ˈputrid
   d. ˈpupil
   e. ˈpugilist
   f. ˈPugilism ˈisn't a ˈsport for the ˌpuny.
   g. The ˈfood was ˈputrid / but the ˈwater ˌpure.
   h. His ˈpupils are reˈputed to ˈget good reˌsults.

4. / bl- /
   a. blow   b. black
   b. blue   c. blench
   c. blood   d. blink
   d. blame   e. blast
   e. blight   f. blot

   g. Their ˈblasphemy was ˌblatant.
   h. ˈBlast them for their ˌblack ˌactions.
   i. ˈSay a ˈblessing for the ˌblind.
   j. The ˈwind ˈblew and ˈblustered all ˌnight.
   k. Her ˈdazzling blue ˈsari made me ˌblink.

Consonant Clusters 177

l. I ˈblench at the ˈsight of ˌblood.
m. My ˈmind went ˈblank and ˈeverything ˈblacked ˌout.
n. ˈBlossoms ˈbloom on ˇsome trees / ˈjust beˈfore the ˌrains.
o. You must ˈblot out the ˈmemory of your ˌblunders.
p. We ˈcan't blame ˇblight / for the ˈpoor ˈcrop ˋthis ˌyear.

5. / br- /

a. bright   f. brown
b. break   g. brook
c. brief   h. broil
d. ˈbrackish   i. brick
e. ˈbrutal   j. brother

k. My ˈbrother ˈbowls ˌleg-breaks.
l. You'll ˈfeel ˈbrighter after ˌbreakfast.
m. The ˈwater in the ˈbrook's ˌbrackish.
n. His ˈbrusqueness ˈseems to ˌbrowbeat ˌpeople.
o. The briˈgade broke ˈthrough on a ˈwide ˌfront.
p. ˈBring me that anˈtique ˈbronze ˋbrooch you ˌbought.
q. ˈWho first ˈbroached the ˈsubject of the ˈBritish withˋdrawal?
r. He was ˈstabbed in a ˈbrief but ˈbrutal ˌbrawl.
s. He's ˌone of the most ˈbrilliant ˈbrains in ˌIndia.
t. He ˈused a ˈbrace and a ˌbit / to ˈfix the ˌbracket.

6. /tr-/

a. try   f. trudge
b. trip   g. trust
c. tread   h. truth
d. trod   i. ˈtrophy
e. tree   j. traˈditional

k. Let's ˈtry another ˌtrip.
l. The ˈtreasurer's ˈjust been trans ˌferred.
m. He ˈplays the ˈtrumpet and tromˌbone.
n. ˈUnder the ˈtemple was a ˌtreasure ˌtrove.
o. There's a ˈtrend aˈway from traˈditional deˌsigns.
p. We've ˈjust ˈbought a ˈnew ˈtractor and ˌtrailer.
q. You should atˈleast ˈtry to ˈtell the ˌtruth.
r. There's a ˈnew transˈlation into ˈHindi of ˈShakespeare's ˌtragedies.
s. We ˈfollowed the ˈtracks to the ˈfoot of a ˌtree.
t. We ˈhope to transˈform our eˈconomy in ˈthis tranˈ sitional ˌperiod.

7. /tj-/
    a. tune
    b. ˈtutor
    c. ˈtumult
    d. ˈtumour
    e. You must ˈwear ˈtunics on ˌTuesday.
    f. The ˈtumult was about tuˌition ˌfees.
    g. The ˈtuba is ˈnot a very ˌtuneful ˌinstrument.

8. / tw /
    a. twin
    b. twelve
    c. ˈtwilight
    d. ˈtwitter
    e. ˈTwist it ˈtwice ˌround.
    f. ˈBirds ˈtwitter and ˈtweet at ˌtwilight.
    g. There were ˈtwelve ˈsets of ˈtwins ˈborn last ˌyear.

9. / dr- /
    a. draw   f. drain
    b. dry   g. dress

c. drop
d. drink
e. draft
h. drown
i. ˈdrama
j. ˈdrastic

k. We ˈdread aˈnother ˈyear's ˌdrought.
l. The ˈdoctor's ˈdrugs ˈmade me ˌdrowsy.
m. The ˈdrama had a ˈdrastic ˌending.
n. The ˈEnglish have a ˈdreadful ˌdrawl.
o. ˈDrink it ˈdown to the ˌdregs.
p. My ˈdraughtsman will ˈdraw up the ˌblueprints.
q. The ˈdrowned ˈwoman was ˈdressed in ˌwhite.
r. There's a ˈterrible ˈdraught in the ˌdrawing room.
s. ˈSomebody ˈdrove the ˈseed ˈdrill into the ˌditch.
t. I was ˈso ˈdry I ˈdrained it to the ˈlast ˌdrop.

10. /dj-/
    a. duke
    b. deuce
    c. ˈduty
    d. duˈress
    e. ˈdurable
    f. 'You're a ˈdeucedly ˈbad ˌplayer', said the ˌduke.
    g. I was ˈcalled to ˈduty for the duˈration of hosˌtilities.

11. / kl- /
    a. clean
    b. climb
    c. clot
    d. clothes
    e. clip
    f. ˈclient
    g. ˈclever
    h. ˈclearing
    i. ˈclassical
    j. ˌkleptoˈmania

    k. ˈRavi ˈclaims he's ˌclever.
    l. The ˈclimate is ˈclearly very ˌtrying.
    m. My ˈclient was ˈpushed off a ˌcliff.
    n. ˈClarify what you ˈsaid about ˈclause ˌfour.

o. ǀClasp your ǀhands and ǀclench your ˌteeth.
p. There was a ǀclanking and ǀclanging of maˌchinery.
q. There are ǀmarks of ˋclaws in the ˌclay.
r. ǀSome people ǀwant to clamp ˋdown on ˌclassical ˌlanguages.
s. The ǀlowest ǀclasses are ǀpoorly ǀclad in ǀworn ˌclothes.
t. A ǀclash of oˌpinion / ǀled to a ˋcleavage in the ˌparty.

12. /kr-/
    a. cream
    b. crore
    c. cross
    d. crouch
    e. crow
    f. Christ
    g. crate
    h. ǀcricket
    i. ǀcrafty
    j. ǀcrooked

    k. ǀCricket's a ˋcrazy ˌgame.
    l. ǀCrabs are ˋqueer ˌcreatures.
    m. The ǀroof's ǀcracked and ǀcrumbling aˌway.
    n. He's a ǀcranky, ˋcrusty ˌkind of ˌperson.
    o. He made ǀcrores of ruǀpees through ǀsheer ˌcraftiness.
    p. You ǀcan't ǀcross the ǀcreek beǀcause of the ˌcrocodiles.
    q. She ǀcried and ǀcried, but ǀno one ˌheard her.
    r. The ǀcrooks ǀtried to ˋhide / ǀcrouching ǀdown behind the ˌcounter.
    s. It was so ǀcrassly ǀstupid as to be ǀbarely ˌcredible.
    t. Go ǀup to the ǀcrest of the ˌhill / and ǀturn ǀright at the ˌcrossroads.

13. /kj-/
    a. cute
    b. queue

c. cure
d. ˈcurious
e. ˈcubicle
f. ˈEachˈcube ˈgives off ˈmany ˈcuries of ˈradioacˌtivity.
g. ˈForm a ˌqueue / and you'll ˈeach ˈget a ˌcubicle.

14. /kw-/
    a. quite
    b. queen
    c. quell
    d. qualms
    e. quick
    f. The ˈriots were ˈquickly ˌquelled.
    g. The ˈqueen ˈquivered with ˌanger.
    h. Beer in ᵛany ˌquantity / ˈmakes some ˈpeople ˌqueasy.
    i. ˈQualms of ˈconscience are ˈquite ˈout of the ˌquestion.

15. /gl-/
    a. glass   f. glum
    b. glow   g. glare
    c. glide   h. glove
    d. glad   i. ˈgleeful
    e. glue   j. ˈglisten
    k. She's ˈgloriously ˌglamorous!
    l. My ˈgloves seemed ˌglued to my ˌhand.
    m. You're ˈalways ˈready with ˈglib and ˈgloating ˌanswers.
    n. You ˈneedn't ˈglorify ˈgluttony when ˈsome are ˌstarving.
    o. I'd be ˈglad if this ˈbook had a ˌglossary.
    p. ˈRam caught a ˈglimpse of the ˈglider before it ˌcrashed.

q. It makes me ˈgloomy to ˈsee you ˈglowering like ˌthat.
r. Her ˈface seemed to ˌglow / in the ˈglare of the ˌfire.
s. The ˈmountain ˌmeadows / ˈgleamed and ˈglistened like ˈglass after the ˈearly ˈmorning ˌdew.
t. He ˈgave me a ˈkind of ˈglazed ˈglance / when I ˈtold him he'd ˈwon the ˌprize.

16. /gr-/
    a. grow
    b. grave
    c. grass
    d. grind
    e. groin
    f. grit
    g. greet
    h. grand
    i. grain
    j. ˈgrotto

    k. The ˈgradient ˈgrows ˈgradually ˌsteeper.
    l. There's a ˈgrowing deˈmand for ˌgrapes.
    m. I'm ˈvery ˈgrateful for the ˌgraphs.
    n. The ˈgrass grows ˈgreenest after the ˌrains.
    o. The ˈsound of a ˈgramophone ˌgreeted us.
    p. My ˈgrandfather's a ˈgreat one for ˌstories.
    q. We have a ˈgrowing ˈsurplus of ˌgraduates.
    r. It's ˈgratifying to ˈsee so much ˌgreenery.
    s. I've a ˈgrievance about my ˈgrain alloˌcation.
    t. Your ˈjokes are groˈtesque as well as ˌgross.

17. /fl-/
    a. flow
    b. flight
    c. fling
    d. flat
    e. fleet
    f. flay
    g. flare
    h. flute
    i. flirt
    j. ˈflimsy

    k. ˈFling him ˈout of the ˌflat.
    l. The ˈfleet is ˈfloating at ˌanchor.

Consonant Clusters

    m. ˈDon't get ˈflustered or ˈflurried unˌnecessarily.
    n. He has a ˈflair for ˌflute ˌplaying
    o. Her ˈcurries have a ˈrather ˈflat ˌflavour.
    p. ˈHalf the ˈart of ˈflirting ˈlies in ˌflattery.
    q. The ˈflare path's ˈlit up for the ˌnight ˌflights.
    r. She ˈlet forth a ˈflow of ˌwords, / so I ˌfled.
    s. ˈAfter the ˈrail diˌsaster / we found ˈflaws in the ˈflange of a ˈwheel.
    t. There was a ˈsudden ˌflash / and then ˈflames flew ˈup into the ˌsky.

18. /fr-/
    a. fright
    b. friend
    c. frame
    d. ˈfrigid
    e. ˈfrantic

    f. My ˈfriend is ˈfrightened of ˌfrogs.
    g. Their ˈfruit ˈsalad was ˈsimply ˌfrightful.
    h. ˇFrankly, / ˈfreedm has to be ˌfought for.
    i. There are ˈfresh ˈreasons for ˈfriction on the ˌfrontier.

19. /fj-/
    a. few
    b. fumes
    c. ˈfutile
    d. ˈfurious
    e. ˈfugitive

    f. ˈNuclear ˈfusion reˌactions / have imˈmense ˈfuel possiˌbilities.
    g. Our ˈfight against the ˈfumes was ˈfutile.
    h. The ˈfugitives were ˈfurious when they were ˌcaught.

20. / θr /
    a. throw   thrive
    b. through   throne
    c. thrust
    d. ˈThrow it through ˌhere.
    e. ˈChildren ˈdon't ˈthrive on ˌthrashings.
    f. That's ˈthree ˋtimes they've ˌthreatened me.

21. /sp-/
    a. spin   f. spite
    b. spank   g. spoke
    c. spur   h. sport
    d. spend   i. spire
    e. speed   j. spoil
    k. You've ˈspoiled my ˌspanner.
    l. ˈEven the specˋtators were ˌspeechless.
    m. Their ˈspokesman said they ˈacted sponˌtaneously.
    n. His ˈbreath came spoˈradically and spasˌmodically.
    o. He's a ˈspendthrift, and a ˋspineless kind of ˌperson.
    p. The oppoˈsition ˈspied on our ˌsports ˌteam.
    q. Her ˈhouse is ˈalways ˈspick and ˌspan
    r. We seem to ˈspend a ˈlot on ˌspices.
    s. Speak ˋup if you've got ˈsomething ˌspecial toˌsay.
    t. The ˈspokes of the ˈwheel ˈspun round at ˈhighˌspeed.

22. /st-/
    a. steal   f. stock
    b. still   g. stole
    c. stung   h. stay
    d. stall   i. sty
    e. stench
    j. The ˈsty ˈstank ˌterribly.

k. 'Moral 'standards have 'started 'going ˌdown.
l. The 'staff seem ˋstale / and 'lack ˌstamina.
m. 'Don't just 'stand ˌstill, / ˌstamp on it!
n. 'Starch is 'no 'good as a 'staple ˌdiet.
o. I 'still don't be'lieve your sta'tistics on starˌvation.
p. We ˋstared at them / as they were 'stark ˌnaked.
q. They 'stole some 'stalks of 'sugarcane from the ˌstall.
r. There's a 'stairway for the ˌstars / to go 'down on to the ˌstage.
s. Put 'saddles and ˋstirrups on the ˌhorses / and 'take them 'out of the ˌstable.

23. / sk- /
   a. skate
   b. skill
   c. skunk
   d. sky
   e. 'scarecrow
   f. 'scanty
   g. 'skier
   h. 'scapegoat
   i. The 'scarecrow 'stood against the ˌskyline.
   j. I was 'cast as a ˋscapegoat in their ˌschemes.
   k. The 'skiers 'skimmed across the 'surface of the ˌsnow.
   l. You get 'scabs on your 'skin if you have ˌscurvy.
   m. We made 'skilful 'use of ˋsky scanning deˌvices / to 'warn us of 'enemy ˌaircraft.

24. / sm- /
   a. smear
   b. small
   c. smoke
   d. 'smitten
   e. smile
   f. smack
   g. smell
   h. smooth
   i. smirk
   j. 'smother
   k. 'All that ˌsmoke / 'made my ˋeyes ˌsmart.
   l. I 'smacked my ˋlips at the deˌlicious ˌsmell.

m. Your exˈpression sugˈgests a ˎsmirk / ˈrather than a ˌsmile.
n. The ˈfire ˈsmouldered for a ˈlong ˎtime / before it was ˌsmothered.
o. The ˈtank went ˈsmack into a ˎwall / and ˈsmashed it into ˌsmithereens

25. / sn- /
    a. snake   d. sneer
    b. sniff   e. snip
    c. snow

    f. I ˈknow I ˎsnore when I ˌsnooze.
    g. ˈStop that ˈsnickering and ˈsniggering at ˌonce.
    h. The ˈdog ˈsniffed the ˈmeat and then ˌsnarled.
    i. ˈSneak round the ˈback and ˈpick off the ˌsniper.

26. / sl /
    a. sleep   d. slot
    b. slow   e. sluice
    c. slay   f. slum
    d. slink   g. ˈslaughter
    e. sly   h. ˈslovenly

    i. She's a ˈslovenly ˌslattern!
    j. ˈSlang isn't ˈnecessarily ˎslipshod ˌlanguage.
    k. ˈSlum ˈclearance is a ˎslow ˌjob.
    l. ˈShare ˈprices ˈslipped catasˎtrophically / during the ˌslump.
    m. I'll ˈsleep the ˈsleep of the ˌjust.
    n. ˈSlide a ˈtwo-rupee ˎcoin into the ˌslot.
    o. ˈSlimness, ˈslightness, and ˌslenderness / mean ˈmuch the ˌsame.
    p. The ˈsloop ˈslid down the ˈslipway into the ˎharbour.

Consonant Clusters

q. They ˈslouch and ˈslink about in such a ˈslothful ˌmanner.
r. When the ˈwater ˈpressure ˌslackened / we ˈclosed the ˌsluice ˌgates.

27. / sw- /

a. swim
b. swear
c. swat
d. swine
e. sweet
f. swerve
g. swank
h. swamp
i. sway
j. swarm

k. The ˈswamp's ˈswarming with ˌwater ˌsnakes.
l. We ˈsweated in the ˈsweltering ˌheat.
m. My ˈboat swept ˈswiftly down the ˌriver.
n. The ˈdriver ˈswerved ˈswiftly to aˈvoid the ˌchild.
o. The ˈswine ˈswindled me ˈout of my ˌproperty!

28. / spr- /

a. sprain
b. sprint
c. spray
d. spread
e. spruce
f. sprout
g. spree
h. ˈspritely

i. The ˈsprinter ˈsprained a ˌligament.
j. Those ˈspruce ˈseedlings are ˈsprouting ˌwell.
k. We ˈspread ᵛfertiliser / and ˈthen ˈsprayed in ˌsecticide.
l. I ˈfeel so ˈspritely I'll ˈgo on the ˌspree.
m. There's a ˈsystem of ˋditches / ˈspreading ˈout from the ˌsprings.

29. / str- /

a. strain
b. stride
f. straw
g. stroke

c. strength h. struck
d. strict i. straight
e. stray j. ˈstranger

k. A ˈstream runs aˈlongside the ˌstreet.
l. The ˈstrangler had the ˈstrength of ˌten.
m. ˈStreamlining it ˈwouldn't make it ˈless ˌstrong.
n. Our deˈmands will be ˈstronger if we ˌstrike.
o. ˈStrictly ˌspeaking / we ˈshouldn't ˈstretch a ˋpoint for you.
p. He ˋstruggled, / so they ˈstrapped him to a ˌstretcher.
q. That ˈbridge ˈstraddling the ˇstraits / has ˈgreat straˈtegic ˌvalue.
r. ˈStrange to ˌsay / I ˈdidn't ˋhear of your ˌstraitened ˌcircumstances.
s. The ˈSherpas seemed to ˈstroll aˈlong with an ˈeasy ˌstride.
t. Our supˈplies of ˌstraw / will ˈstretch out a ˈfew weeks ˌmore.

30. / skr- /

a. scream f. scroll
b. scrawl g. scrounge
c. screw h. scrub
d. script i. ˈscramble
e. scribe j. ˈscrupulous

k. The ˈdogs were ˈscrambling for ˌscraps.
l. ˌEven the ˈscrapbooks were ˈcarefully ˌscrutinised.
m. Use ˈscrews for the ˈhinges of the ˌscreen.
n. You can ˈscribble on the ˈmargin of your ˌscript.
o. ˈWhat's ˋthat / ˈscrawled in the ˈcorner of the ˌscroll?
p. He's got ˈno ˈscruples about ˈscrounging what he ˌcan.

q. The ˈcry was ˈsomething between a ˈscreech and a ˌscream.

31. /skw-/
    a. squeeze
    b. square
    c. squirm
    d. squat
    e. squint
    f. His ˈsquint's so ˈbad it ˈmakes me ˌsquirm.
    g. ˈEveryone ˈclaimed ˈsquatter's ˈrights over a ˈsmall ˈsquare of ˌland.
    h. The ˈfledgelings ˈsqueaked and ˈsquawked aˈway until they were ˌfed.
    i. Conˈditions in the ˌbustees / are ˈso ˌsqualid / even ˈI ˈfeel ˌsqueamish.

32. / hj- /
    a. huge
    b. ˈhumid
    c. huˈmane
    d. ˈhumour
    e. There's a ˈhuge ˈincrease in huˌmidity toˌday.
    f. His ˈhumour is ˈcruel / rather than huˌmane.

33. / mj- /
    a. mute
    b. ˈmusic
    c. ˈmural
    d. muˈseum
    e. The muˈseum ˈspecialises in ˈold ˈmusical ˌinstruments.
    f. I ˈstood ˈmute in admiˈration before the ˌmurals.

34. / nj- /
    a. news
    b. ˈneutral
    c. ˈneuter
    d. neuˈrosis
    e. I've got neuˈritis, / ˈnot a neuˌrosis.
    f. ˈIs there any ˈnews about the ˌneutral ˌpowers?

Final Clusters

1. /-tjt/
   a. lurched
   b. reached
   c. botched
   d. beached
   e. searched
   f. matched
   g. fetched
   h. bleached
   i. ditched
   j. at'tached

   k. 'When they ˌfetched, it, / we 'ditched the 'whole iˌdea.
   l. We 'reached the con'clusion the 'teams were 'well ˌmatched.
   m. I 'flinched as the 'truck 'lurched across the ˌroad.
   n. The 'job was 'botched through ˌyour being atˌtached to us.
   o. The 'boats will have to be ˎwatched when they're ˌbeached.

2. / -ft /
   a. thrift
   b. graft
   c. tuft
   d. soft
   e. laughed
   f. coughed
   g. draught
   h. left
   i. loft
   j. be'reft

   k. The 'job was so 'soft I ˌlaughed.
   l. The 'raft didn't 'drift as 'far as exˌpected.
   m. Re'turns from 'thrift are leˌgitimate, / from 'graft ˌnot so.
   n. There was 'such an 'icy ˌdraught / I 'almost 'coughed my ˌlungs up.

3. / -kst /
   a. axed
   d. mixed

b. boxed
c. hoaxed
e. re'laxed

f. My ˈpost was ˈaxed when the ˈschools were ˌmixed.
g. If we ˈhadn't re ˌlaxed / we'd ˈnever have been ˌhoaxed.

4. / -skt /
   a. risked
   b. asked
   c. husked
   d. frisked
   e. masked

   f. The ˈmasked ˈbandits ˈfrisked our ˌpockets.
   g. I ˈasked them ˈwhy they ˈrisked their ˌlives.

5. / -ld /
   a. killed
   b. held
   c. reeled
   d. fold
   e. bald
   f. filled
   g. cold
   h. mild
   i. called
   j. soiled

   k. The ˈsheep are held ˈpenned in the ˌfold.
   l. The ˈroom was ˈfilled with ˈbald-headed ˌmen.
   m. A ˈcold ˈspell was ˈfollowed by a ˌmild one.
   n. He ˈcalled ˈout as he ˈreeled ˈdrunkenly across the ˌroom.
   o. His ˈbody's so ˌcold / he ˈmust have been ˈkilled some ˌtime ago.

6. / -sk /
   a. task
   b. tusk
   c. risk
   d. husk
   e. brusque
   f. frisk
   g. brisk
   h. mosque
   i. ask
   j. musk

k. ˈAsk how ˈmuch the ˌtusk is.
l. The ˈcask is ˈfull of ˌmusk.
m. There's a ˈrisk in ˈbeing too ˌbrusque.
n. Your ˈtask is to ˈmake ˈtrade ˌbrisk.
o. I ˈleft my ˈflask in the ˌmosque.

7. / -ks /
   a. seeks
   b. books
   c. cakes
   d. likes
   e. backs
   f. box
   g. talks
   h. drinks
   i. bakes
   j. ˈrucksacks

   k. She ˈlikes ˌcakes.
   l. He ˈalways ˈtalks about his ˌbooks.
   m. ˈBikes have ˋtwo ˌwheels / and ˈtrikes ˌthree.
   n. The ˈGreeks and ˈTurks are ˈhaving ˌtalks.
   o. We've ˈused ˋhooks/on the ˈbacks of the ˌfrocks.

13. Conversations

Using the conversations

The conversations are intended to provide models of good English, spoken at a level of international intelligibility. They can be used in various ways, as follows.

Listening and repetition

Listen to a conversation on the SmartApp and then read aloud from the book. It is recommended that for this exercise the conversation should first be sectioned, i.e. dealt with in sections.

Guided role play – pair work

Again, listen to the SmartApp, but one person reads from the text while the other improvises his or her role without further recourse to the book. Again the conversation should be sectioned.

Improvised drama

Students should read and/or listen to a conversation, and make notes on its stages and contents. These can be used as the basis for an improvised drama, without further recourse to the text. Students can use the same context, or modify it, e.g. in the conversation 'At the Doctor's' a different illness can be diagnosed. In 'At the Supermarket', Vimala and her mother could make some purchases, or there could be a problem with change at the checkout. Other examples will no doubt spring to mind.

1. At the Supermarket

Context: Vimala, her mother, Mrs Chakravarti, and a British friend, Jennifer are at the entrance to a large supermarket near Mumbai. Mrs Chakravarti comes from a small town in Central India, and this is her first visit to such an establishment.

Vimala, her mother Mrs. Chakravarti, her friend Jennifer.

V : 'Come on then ˌmother, 'let's goˋin. /This'll be aˈnew exˋperience for you.

C : It ˈcertainly ˋwill. / Even the ˈcar ˈpark is eˌnormous. / There's ˈnothing like ˈthis at ˌhome.

V : ˈLet me introˈduce a ˈnew ˌfriend / ˌJennifer. She's on seˈcondment to our ˌcompany.

J : I'm ˈvery ˈglad to ˋmeet you, Mrs. ˌChakravarti.

C : ˈWe ˈused to ˈgo to you ˈpeople for eduˌcation, and ˈnow ˈyou come to ˋus. That's ˇprogress, I supˌpose

J : I exˈpect things ˈeven out in the ˌend.

V : The ˈidea beˈhind a ˌsupermarket / is that ˈpeople do ˈall their ˈshopping under ˈone ˌroof.

C : So you ˈhave to have a ˋcar / to ˌcome here?

V : ˋYes, / unˈless you ˈlive ˈclose ˌby. But the ˈnumber of ˈpeople with ˇcars in ˌIndia / has ˈgrown eˋnormously in ˌrecent ˌyears, / as you ˌknow.

They pass inside.

C : ˈWhat are those ˋthings over ˌthere, / ˈwhere ˈpeople are ˇqueuing up / with their ˈbaskets on ˌwheels?

V : ˈThose are the ˋtills, / where you ˌpay, / and the ˈgirls beˇhind them / are the ˋcheckout girls.

C : Well, it ˈall ˈlooks very ˈclean and ˌmodern, / a bit ˋtoo modern, / if you ˌask me. ˈWhat are these ˌpackages

ˌhere, / in ˈthis ˌcabinet, / they ˈseem as if they're being ˈkept ˋfrozen.
V : They're ready - ˋmade ˌmeals, ˌMummy.
C : ˈReady-made ˌmeals? / Your ˈfather would ˈnever have put ˋup with ready ˌmeals. You ˈmean you can ˈbuy ˈfood that's alˈready been ˌcooked?
V : Well, you have to ˈheat it up in the ˌmicrowave. You should ᵛrealise, Mummy, / that Saˈtish and I both ˋ work. We ˈdon't have ˈtime to ˈdo eˈlaborate ˋcooking, / exˈcept at weekˋends, / and ˈsometimes ˈnot even ˌthen.
C : And ˈwhat are these ˈwhite ˌlabels / on these ˈpackaged ˈpieces of ˌchicken?
V : They'reᵛsell-by dates, Mummy. The ˈsupermarket guaranˈtees to ˈsell ˌthings by a ˈcertain ˌdate, / or it will ˈtake them ˈoff the ˌshelves.
C : My ˈfriend Mrs. ˈGurumurthy ᵛtold me about those. She ˈsays that ˈsometimes the ˈsupermarket will ˈtake off the ˋold ˌlabel, / if the ˈarticle is ˈgetting ˈclose to its exᵛpiry ˌdate, / and ˈsubstitute a ˋnew one.
V : I'm ˈsure that ˈwouldn't ˈhappen ˋhere. It ˈwouldn't be in the ᵛsupermarkets' ˌinterest / to ˈgive their ˈcustomers ˋ food ˌpoisoning.
C : And aˌnother thing, / ˈwhat ˈhappened to ˈall the ˈsmall ˋshops round ˌhere? Have their ˈowners just ˋvanished into ˈthin ˌair?
J : ˈSupermarkets creˈate ˈjobs as ˌwell, / but ˈone thing ˌcertain / is that they're ˈnot ˈjobs for the ˈpeople who have been diˋsplaced. / They're supˈposed to be emˈployment ᵛneutral, I believe the ˌphrase ˌis, / in the ˈsad ˈlanguage of Ecoˋnomics. But there is ˈsomething of the Surˈvival of the ˋFittest about it, / I aˌgree. ˈOne soˈlution is ᵛheld to ˌbe / that ˈsmall ˈshops should ˌspecialise / and ˈmove ˌupmarket, / but I'm ˈnot conˌvinced.

C : ⁺I've been ⁺specialising for some ˌtime. / I ⁺buy ⁺fresh ⁺fish from the ˎtanks, / ⁺caught that ˌmorning. / I'll ⁺wager ⁺this ⁺supermarket ⁺can't ˎbeat ˌthat.

Glossary

secondment : the practice of sending an employee from one company to another for a period, usually for training or to gain expertise.

enormously : greatly

checkout girl : the person at the exit to a store who takes your money or processes your credit card.

microwave : microwave oven, a kitchen appliance which cooks food quickly using microwave radiation.

sell-by date : the date after which an item of food should not be sold.

employment neutral : creating as many jobs as it destroys.

2. In a ˈRailway ˌCarriage

A : Do you ˈknow if this ˈtrain ˈstops at ˌDaulatabad?
B : ˈNo, / I ˈdon't ˈthink so. It ˈgoes straight ˈthrough to Manˌmad.
A : But they ˈtold me at Auˈrangabad that it ˈdid...
B : ˈWho told you?
A : The ˈman at the ˈticket ˌbarrier.
B : They ˈdon't ˈknow what they're ˈdoing ˌnowadays. Misˈ leading the ˌpublic; / ˈthat's what it ˌis. ˈWhat're you ˈgoing to ˈdo?
A : ˈGo on to Manˌmad / and ˈcatch the ˈnext train ˈback I supˌpose.
B : You'll ˈhave to ˈwait till toˇmorrow, / there ˈisn't anˈother to ˈnight.
A : My ˈwife'll be ˈworried to ˈdeath. She was exˈpecting me ˈback.
B : ˈIsn't the ˌrest of your ˌfamily ˌthere?
A : ˈNo;/ we've ˈjust ˈmoved. My ˈparents and ˈbrothers and ˈsisters are ˈcoming on ˈlater.
B : There's a ˈrest ˈhouse at Manˈmad ˌstation. You ˈmight get a ˌbed.
A : ˈYes, / and be ˈput to a ˈlot of exˌpense, / ˈall because the ˈrailway ˈdoesn't ˈknow its ˈown ˌtimetable.
B : ˈHere's the ˈticket exˌaminer. Let's ˈsee what ˈhe's ˌgot to ˌsay.
A : ˈTicket exˌaminer, / ˈwhy doesn't this ˈtrain ˈstop at ˌDaulatabad?
T.E : I ˈbeg your ˌpardon, sir?
A : I ˌsaid ' ˈWhy doesn't this ˈtrain ˈstop at ˌDaulatabad?'
T.E : But it's ˈnot supˈposed to, sir. It ˈnever ˌstops at ˌDaulatabad.

B : Then ˈwhy did ˈone of your ˈpeople at Auˌrangabad / ˈtell this ˈgentleman that it ˌdid?
I.E : I ˈdon't ˎknow, sir. I'm ˈvery ˇsorry. He ˈmust have ˈmade a misˎtake.
A : ˊMust have? You're ˈtelling me he ˎmust have. I ˈthink I'll ˈsend the ˌRailway / a ˈbill for my ˈextra exˎpenses.
T.E : You could ˈalways ˈwrite a ˈletter of comˇplaint, ˌsir.
B : It ˈwouldn't ˈdo him ˈany ˎgood, / it would ˈonly disapˈpear into your ˌfiles.
A : ˎLook, / we're ˈcoming into ˈDaulatabad ˇnow. When I ˈthink I could be ˈhome in ˈten ˎminutes!
B : ˎWait a ˌminute, / the ˈtrain's ˈslowing ˌdown.
A : We've ˈalmost ˎstopped.
T.E : There's a ˎsignal aˌgainst us. We'll ˈgo on in a ˌminute.
A : Well, you'll ˈgo on wiˈthout me. I'm ˈjumping ˎout.
T.E : But ˈthat's aˈgainst the reguˇlations, ˌsir. You ˈmight get ˌhurt.
A : You ˈknow what you can ˈdo with your regulˌations. ˌOut of my way, / ˎquick. Goodˇbye. (He ˌleaves.)
T.E : Be ˇcareful, ˌsir.

3. The Sharma's Party

Context : Entertainment is part of business life. The type of entertainment could be formal, a dinner for example, or a relatively formal or informal party. The choice will depend to some extent on the seniority of the chief guest, if there is one. If the guests are of equal status, or just friends, then informality is more likely. The Sharma's party, judging from the guest list, is likely to be on the formal side.

Mr Sharma : ˈDid I ˌtell you / that Mr. ˈJain from ˈhead ˌoffice/ was ˈpaying us a ˌvisit?
Mrs Sharma : ˇYes /I beˈlieve you ˎdid mention it. ˈWhat's he ˎcoming for?
Mr S : ˈNobody ˈreally ˎknows, / but I exˈpect it's ˈsome kind of insˎpection. He ˈvisits ˈall the ˈbranches from ˈtime to ˌtime.
Mrs S : ˈWhy don't they ˈlet you ˈknow what it's ˈall aˌbout?
Mr S : I supˈpose the ˇtheory is / we'll be ˈmore on our ˌtoes / if we ˈdon't ˈknow what's in ˎstore for us. ˎAnyway, / I'd ˈlike to ˈgive a ˎparty for him. I ˈthink he'll exˎpect it.
Mrs S : ˊWhat? ˊWhen did you ˌsay he was ˌcoming?
Mr S : I ˎtold you. In ˈfour days' ˌtime.
Mrs S : And you exˌpect me / to ˈlay on a ˈdecent ˈparty at ˈsuch ˈshort ˌnotice? You must be ˎmad.
Mr S : I'm ˎsorry, ˌdear, / but I've ˈonly ˈjust ˎthought about it.
Mrs S : It'll be the ˎusual thing. The ˈpeople we'd ˇlike to come / will have ˈother enˌgagements / and the ˈones we ˇdon't ˈwant / will ˈflock here in ˎhordes.
Mr S : Let's ˈdraw up a ˈlist of ˎpossibles / and ˈthen you'd ˈbetter ˈget on the ˎphone.

Mrs S : Oh, ˈall ˌright. There's the Colˈlector and his ˌwife / and the ˈman in ˈcharge of the ˌradio ˌstation / and that ˈnice ˎParsi ˌfamily. ˈWhat about that Taxˎation man?

Mr S : ˎNo,/ notˎhim. He ˈmakes me ˈfeel ˎguilty. The ˈold ˎRaja might ˌcome. He's a comˈplete ˇidiot / but he's ˈquite ˎgood ˌsocially.

Mrs S : So ˈlong as he ˈdoesn't go ˈon about the ˈgood old ˈdays ˈall theˌtime. There's the ˎforeign comˌmunity, of ˌcourse.

Mr S : ˎYes, / but ˈnot too ˎmany. ˈMost of them ˎdrink ˌfar too ˌmuch / and ˈthen they ˈget obˎjectionable.

Mrs S : Oh, I ˈdon't ˌknow. I ˈknow at least ˈone ˈtolerable Aˎmercian. The ˈone who ˈworks at the Uniˈversity Obˎservatory. Then there's that ˈnice ˈRussian engiˎneer and his ˌwife.

Mr S : You'd ˈbetter ˈkeep ˇthem / in ˈseparate ˈcorners of theˌroom. ˈWhat about the ˎMorrisons?

Mrs S : ˈNot at ˎany price. I mean ˎhe's ˌrather a ˌsweetie / but when you ˈlisten to ˇher / you'd ˈthink the ˈBritish had ˈnever ˈleft ˎIndia. And, those ˈawful ˎclothes she ˌwears.

Mr S : ˈAll ˌright, / ˎno ˌMorrisons. (A ˈknock isˌheard. Mr. ˈS looks ˈout of theˌwindow.)

Mr S : Huˌllo, / it's a ˎtelegram. I'll ˈgo and ˈsee what it's aˌbout. (Heˌleaves, / then ˈre-ˌenters.)

Mr S : It's from Mr. ˌJain. He's putting ˈoff his ˈvisit for ˈthreeˌmonths.

4. A ʹTalk about the ˌFuture

Context: In most families with adolescent sons and daughters there will be discussion about future careers. In some cases, parents and children may not totally agree.

Father : Viˊnayak!
V : ˋYes, ˌfather.
F : ʹIsn't it ˌtime / you deʹcided ʹwhat you were ʹgoing to ˌdo?
V : ˋYes, / I supʹpose it ˌis, ˌfather.
F : Well, ʹwhat are your ˋplans?
V : I ʹhaven't ʹreally ˋgot any, ˌfather. I ʹhaven't ˋthought very ˌmuch aˌbout it.
F : Well, it's ʹtime you ˋdid. ʹAfter ˌall, / your final year in interᵛmediate / beʹgins ʹnext ˌterm. You must ʹhave ˋsome ˌpreferences by ˌnow.
V : I ʹquite ʹfancy ˋmedicine, / but then the ʹgovernment would ʹprobably ˌsend me / to some ʹdreary proˌvincial ˌtown.
F : For the ʹvery good ᵛreason / that ʹthat's where ʹdoctors are ˌneeded. ʹYou ʹyoung ʹpeople are ʹtoo ʹfond of ˋcity life. ˋAnyway, / are your ʹscience ʹsubjects ˌgood enˌough?
V : They're about ˋaverage, / and my ʹmaths is ʹquite ˌgood.
F : ʹWhat about the ʹI.A. ˋS.
V : ʹToo much ˋform ˌfilling ˌin / and ʹsitting behind a ˋdesk all ˌday.
F : ˋRubbish. A ʹgood Colʹlector should be ʹout and aʹbout a ˋlot/ ˋhelping his ʹdistrict's deˌvelopment.
V : Well, I must ʹonly have ʹmet the ˋbad ones.
F : ʹDon't be ʹso disresˋpectful. You ʹdon't ʹknow what you're ˋtalking about.
V : ʹWhat I'd ᵛreally ˌlike to ˌdo / is ʹstudy aˋbroad.

F : ˈIsn't ˈIndia ˌgood enough ˌfor you?
V : ˋYes,/ of ˋcourse it is, / but I ˈdon't think ˈtravel does ˈany ˈharm ˋeither. ˋAnyway, / ˈlook at the ˈjobs people ˈget who've ˈbeen overˋseas.
F : Beˈfore you ˈstart ˈthinking aboutˌ that / you'll ˈhave to have a ˈfirst-class B.ˌA. / and a ˈfirst - class ˋM.A., / and ˈeven ˈthen you ˈmay not ˋget there. The compeˈtition is ˈvery ˋfierce for these ˌforeign ˌscholarships.
V : ˈHow about ecoˋnomics, ˌfather? I could ˈuse my ˋmaths there, / on the sta ˋtistical ˌside, and I'm good at IT.
F : I ˈdon't underˋstand it but ˈnow at ˌlast / you're beˈginning to put ˈforward your ˈown iˋdeas, / which is what I ˈlike to ˋsee. If you ˈdid ˈwell in ecoˌnomics / you could ˈjoin one of the ˈbig ˋcompanies / or ˈgo into the Adminisˋtration / or acaˋdemic ˌlife.
V : Yes, I supˈpose there are a ˈlot of ˌopenings.
F : ˈMind ˌyou, / you'll ˈhave to ˈspend a ˈlot ˈless ˈtime in ˌ cafes / or ˈhanging around ˈstreet ˌcorners / than ˋnow. You must get ˋdown to some ˈgood ˈsolid ˋreading.
V : ˈAll ˌright, / ˈhow about ˈtaking out a subˈscription to the ˈˈIndian Eˋconomist' for me?

5. At the Call Centre

Context: Modern banking can be both international and global. Depending on local regulations, one can live in one country, have a bank account (legally) in another, and for queries about the account to be dealt with in a third, from a call centre. Many call centres are located in India. In this dialogue Mr Browne is at first talking to a recorded voice.

Recorded voice : This is SFB＼C. / In ˈorder to ˈhelp us ˈdeal with your ˈcall ˌquickly / ˈplease ˈenter yourˈ 8 ˈdigit client ＼ reference ˌnumber./

Mr Browne : ˌDamn it, / ˈwhere is the ˌthing?/ I ˈhad it ˈhere a ˌmoment ago.

RV : I'm ˌsorry, / I ˈdon't seem to have ˈhad your reˌply. / ˈPlease ˈenter your ˈ 8 ˈdigit ˈclient ＼reference ˌnumber. /

Mr B : ＼Got it. ˈHere we ˌgo. /

Pause

RV : ＼Thank you. /Now ˈplease ˈenter the ˈlast ˈthree ˌdigits/ of your ˈOffshore Accˌount ˌnumber.

Mr B : They ˈdrive you ˌcrazy these ˌpeople./

Pause

RV : And ＼finally, /the ˈlast ˈtwo ˈdigits of your se＼curity ˌnumber. /

Mr B : ˈNow ˌwhat? /

RV : If you ˈwant to ˈknow the ˇbalances in your acˌcounts, / ˈpress ＼1. / If you are ˈmaking a ˇcredit card enˌquiry,/ ˈpress ＼2. / If you have a ＼technical ˌproblem, / ˈpress ＼3. /If you ˈwant to ˈspeak to a ˈcustomer ˇservice repreˌsentative, / ˈpress ＼4./

Mr B : Which ＼is it, for ˌGod's ˌsake? / I'll try ˌ4.

Music
RV : Please ˌhold, / we're ˈtrying to conˌnect you.

Music
RV : Please ˌhold, / we're ˈtrying to conˌnect you.

Music
Manjula HulˈIo. / Mr ˌBrowne, ˈisn't it? / ˈGood ˋday to you, sir. /ˈFirst of all ˈmight I ˈask you a ˈcouple of seˋcurity ˌquestions?
Mr B : ˊWhat? / ˌMore ˌquestions?
M : It will ˈonly ˈtake a ˋmoment, sir. /ˌFirst, yourˈ date of ˌbirth./
Mr B : Well, at ˈleast I ˈknow ˌthat. /The ˈsixteenth of ˌMarch 193ˌ8.
M : And ˇfinally, / the ˈtown where the ˈbirth was ˌregistered.
Mr B : ˋSurbiton.
M : Could you ˌspell that, sir?
Mr B : S-U-R-B-I-T-O-N, ˋSurbiton.
M : That's in ˇEngland, ˌis it sir?
Mr B : ˈYes, it ˌis. At least it ˇwas the ˌlast ˌtime I was ˌthere. You ˈnever ˇknow ˌnowadays.
M : And ˈhow can I ˌhelp you toˌday, Mr ˌBrowne?
Mr B : You ˈknow, you ˈpeople have been ˈtrying to perˋsuade your customers, like ˌme, / to ˇdownload our ˌmonthly ˌstatements/ˈrather than ˈhave them ˈcome through the ˌPost, / on the ˈspurious ˌgrounds/ that this will ˈsave ˌpaper / and will / ˈtherefore be ˈgood for the enˌvironment./ ˈWhat you ˇshould say/ is that ˈyou, the ˌbank / will ˈsave ˌpaper / but ˈwe, the ˇcustomers will ˈuse ˌmore,/ if we ˈprint out our ˌstatements,/ which ˈnaturally we ˋwould ˌdo. / Howeˇver, / I ˈsigned up for ˌthis, / but the ˈsystem ˈdoesn't ˋwork for me.

M : I'm ˈsorry to ˎhear that./ ˈWhat ˌhappened?
Mr B : Well, I can ˈget into the ˈe-statement ˈprogramme OˌKˌ/ but then I'm ˈstopped in my ˌtracks/ because my / ˈp.c. ˌtells me / there's been a ˌsystems ˌfailure.
M : We've been inˈstalling some ˈnew ˌsoftware ˌrecently, sir, / and there have been ˈone or two ˈteething ˌdifficulties. If I ˈmight ˈmake a sugˌgestion, / ˈtry during an ˈoff peak ˌperiod. / In the ˎmean ˌtime, / we'll be ˈworking on the ˌproblem. /
Mr B : And ˈwhen might an ˎoff-peak ˌperiod ˌbe?
M : ˈWhere are you ˎspeaking from, ˌsir?
Mr B : From ˌUruguay, / in South AˌmericaˌA.
M : ˈOne ˌmoment, / I'll ˈlook it ˌup. / Here we ˌare. / You're ˈfour ˈhours beˈhind ˈWestern EuroˌpeanˌtimeˌA,/ ˈEight o'ˈclock in the ˈevening, ˇyour ˌtime. / should be ˌgood.
Mr B : Well, I'll ˎtry it, / but wiˈthout any ˈgreat enˈthusiasm. / But ˈwhat about ˌyou?
M : I'm ˊsorry?
Mr B : ˈWhere are you ˎspeaking from?
M : From BangaˌloreˌA, in ˈSouth ˌIndia.
Mr B : Bangaᵛlore, eh? I ˈspent a ˎweek there once, / about ˈforty ˎyears ago. It was a ˈvery ˎnice ˌcity, / but I exˈpect there have been ˈmany ˌchanges.
M : I exˈpect there ˌhave, sir. / We are ˈnow a ˈworld ˌcentre / for IˌT.
Mr B : A ˌquestion then. If ˈI'm in ˈSouth AˌmericaˌA and ˈyou're in South ᵛIndia, / ˈwhere's my ˌmoney?
M : Your acˈcounts are ˈbased in ˌJersey, sir, / in the ˈChannel ˌIslands. /
Mr B : Well, I'll ˈtake your ˎword for it, / but I ˈwouldn't be surˌprised / if it's ˈlost in ˎCyberspace, / if ˈthat's the ˌphrase. / ˎAnyway, / nice ˎtalking to you / in the ˌend.

M : Is there ¹anything ¹else we can ᵛhelp you with today, Mr ₁Browne?
Mr B : ¹No ₂thank you. / My ¹nerves have been ¹shattered e∖nough for ₁one ₁day.
M : Well, good ¹bye then, Mr ₂Browne.

Glossary
digit : a single client reference number, the confidential number which a bank customer must produce as proof of identity
offshore account : an account not held in the account holder's country of residence
security number : another number used as proof of identity
download : i.e. from the internet
spurious : false
e-statement : electronic bank statement
p.c. : personal computer
software : computer programmes
off-peak : period of minimal use, the opposite of rush hour
IT : information technology
Cyberspace : the electronic universe
shattered : broken

6. At the ˇTravel ˌAgent's

Context: Many people reserve seats on planes and trains with a travel agent, although it is not always as straightforward as one might think. Travel agents are also used for booking holiday accommodation, where the agent might be expected to have specialist knowledge. However, more and more these days, people are making their own reservations on the Internet, thus saving a little money.

Mr Ghosh: ˈCould you get me a reˈturn ˈticket to ˌMumbai, please?
    Travel Agent: ˇCertainly, sir. ˈTwo tier A/ˈC?
G   : ˇYes. ˈWhat time does the ˈtrain ˌleave?
T.A.: At ˈseven in the ˌevening; / you'll be in ˌMumbai / ˈearly the ˈfollowing afterˌnoon. ˈWhen do you ˈwant to ˇgo?
G   : In ˈthree days' ˇtime; / on ˇThursday.
T.A.: That's ˈrather ˈshort ˌnotice. I'd ˈbetter just ˈphone the ˌstation . . . / ˈHulˌlo . . . / Is ˈthat the reserˌvations ˌOffice? . . . ˈGood ˇmorning . . . Have you ˈgot a ˈtwo ˈtier A/C ˈberth to ˈMumbai on ˈThursday, the ˈtwenty / fifth? . . . ˈWhat's ˌthat? ˇYes, / ˇthis month . . . /ˇWhat? Iˈcan't ˇhear you . . .
ˇYes, / ˈall ˌright / I'll ˈring you ˌback...
ˇNo, / I'm ˇsorry, ˌsir. They're ˈfull ˌup.
G   : Whatˈever ˇfor? There's ˇusually ˌplenty of ˌroom.
T.A.: It ˈseems there's a poˈlitical ˇconference ˌon. The ˈlocal ˈparty's made a ˈblock ˌbooking.
G   : Which they ˈmay not ˈtake ˌup. ˇOh well, / there's ˈnothing to be ˇdone about it. ˈWhat about the ˇfollowing day?
T.A.: They ˈsaid at the ˈstation that ˇthat was all ˌright.
Oh I for ˌgot, / ˈwhen did you ˈwant to come ˌback?
G   : On the ˈnext ˈThursday but ˌone, / in ˈtwo weeks' ˌtime.

T.A.: There ˈshouldn't be any ˈproblem ˌthere / but I'll ˈring the ˈstation aˈgain and conˌfirm it.

G : ˈThank you. I'll ˈsend someone ˈround for my ˈtickets this afterˌnoon, / if I ˌmay?

T.A.: ˈCertainly, sir.

G : Oh, ˈcan I get ˈmeals on that ˌtrain?

T.A.: ˈYes, / there's a ˈfull ˈrestaurant ˌservice, / vegeˈtarian and ˈnon-vegeˌtarian.

G : ˈGood. Now I supˈpose I'd ˈbetter ˈpay you.

T.A.: ˈJust as you ˈlike, sir, / either ˌnow / or ˈlater.

G : I'll ˈsettle up ˌnow. ˈHow much do you ˌwant?

T.A.: ˈThree ˈthousand ruˈpees please. I'll ˈwrite you out a reˌceipt.

G : ˈHere you ˈare then.

T.A.: ˈThank you. And ˈhere's the reˌceipt.

G : ˈWhile I'm ˌhere, / there's aˈnother thing. Do you ˈknow anything about ˈhill-stations in the Hiˌmalayas? My ˈfamily ˈwant me to ˈtake them ˈup there in ˌsummer.

T.A.: I could ˈgive you some ˇbrochures.

G : No, I ˈdon't mean ˈthat. ˈHow do I get ˈhold of a ˈreasonable ˌhouse?

T.A.: We ˈknow of a ˈvery good ˈagent in the ˌarea. I ˈwouldn't say his ˈhouses are ˇcheap, / but he's comˈpletely reˌliable.

G : ˈGood. Will you ˈsend him my adˌdress?

T.A.: ˈCertainly. I'm ˈsure you'll ˈfind him ˈmost satisˌfactory.

Glossary

straightforward : without complications

block booking : a reservation for a large number of seats or places

brochure : illustrative material, e.g. on a particular holiday resort

7 Turbulence

Context: Mukesh, a businessman, and Poonam, a psychologist, are on an Air India international flight. Mukesh does not like flying.

Mukesh, Poonam, voice of Air Hostess.
M : ˈWell, ˈsmooth ˌsailing so ˌfar, / ˈthank ˌGod. ˈSorry, ˈwrong ˌmetaphor, I should have said ˈsmooth ˈflying.
P : ˌWhy, / ˈdon't you ˌlike flying?
M : I ˌhate it. I have to ˌdo it, / but it ˌterrifies me. I'm ˈone of ˈthose ˌpeople / who believe that if ˈGod had inᵛtended us to ˌfly / he'd have given us ˌwings.
P : ˈAir ˈIndia has a ˈpretty ˈgood ˈsafety ᵛrecord you ˌknow. You're ˈmore ˈlikely to be ˈkilled by a ˈDelhi ˌtaxi, / if you go to ᵛDelhi, that is.
M : I ˌknow all ˌthat, / but it's ˈabstract ˌthinking. It ˈdoesn't ˈhelp me with my ˈfeelings of ˈsheer ˌunadulterated ˌfright.
P : Well, at ˈleast you can ᵛtalk about them, / which should ˌhelp.
M : ˈWhat about ˌyou though?
P : I can ˈhonestly ˈsay that it ˈdoesn't ˈworry me at ˌall. I ˈhaven't ˈflown very ᵛmuch though.
M : Lucky ˌyou.
P : I believe that some of the ˈbigger ˌairports / ˈhave ˈnow got ˈflying ˈphobia ˌcentres. They have ˈmock-ups of ˌplanes / and you ˈgo in ˈone little ˈstep at a ˌtime / and ˈsit through something that deˈvelops into a simulation of a ˈreal ˌflight. It's supˈposed to ˈwork quite ˌwell. I ˈread an ˌarticle about it ˌsomewhere. You should ˈplan a ˌcourse before ˌthe ˈnext ˌtime you ˌtravel by ˌair.
M : ˈThanks, I ˌwill, / although my ˈfirm will ˈthink I'm a ˌwimp.

H : Will ˈall ˈpassengers ˈplease reˈturn to their ˌseats. The ˈcaptain inˈforms me that we are ˈentering an ˈarea of ˋturbulence.

M : ˈOh ˈLord, / ˈjust when I was beˈginning to reˌlax. You know a ˈlarge ˈpart of the ˌproblem / is that I ˈfeel I've comˈpletely ˈlost conˋtrol of the situˌation.

P : ˈWhich inˈdeed you ˋhave. It's ˈnot the ˈsame as ˈdriving a ˌcar, / alˈthough with ˈthat there's ˈonly an iˌllusion of conˌtrol. When a ˈcar ˈaccident ˌhappens, / then ˈsomeone has usually ˌlost conˌtrol. Do you want to ˈhear my ˈtheory about ˌturbulence?

M : ˌYes, / ˈplease, ˈkeep ˌtalking. It ˈhelps me forˈget where I ˌam.

P : I ˈthink ˈturbulence ˈhappens when we ˈcross a ˈland-sea ˌboundary. ˈCurrents of ˌair, / ᵛthermals if you ˌlike, / ˈrise more ˈquickly from ˋhot ˌland / than they ˈdo from a ˈcool ˌsea. ˌAnyway / ˈthings seem to be ˈsettling down / ˌnow. The 'ˈfasten your ˈseat ˈbelt' ˌsigns have been ˈswitched ˌoff.

M : ˋYou ˈcertainly seem to ˈknow what you're ˋtalking about. ˈWhat ˈjob do you ˌdo, / if you ˈdon't mind my ˌasking?

P : ˈNot at ˋall. I'm a Diˈsaster ˌCounsellor.

M : A ╱what?

P : A Diˋsaster ˌCounsellor. I'm a psyˋchologist. I ˈhelp ˈtraumatised ˈpeople who have been in ˌaccidents, / or whose ˈrelatives have been in ˌfatal acˌcidents.

M : ˈIsn't that a bit ˌmorbid?

P : I ˈdon't ᵛthink so. I ˈfeel it's a useful ˌjob. The ˈmain ᵛproblem is / ˈgetting enough ˈtime to ˈdo it ˌproperly.

M : Well, if ˈever ˋI'm inˌvolved in a diˌsaster / I ˈknow who to look ˋout for.

Glossary

metaphor : figurative or non-literal expression

unadulterated : pure

phobia : irrational fear

mock up : a life size non-working model

wimp : a person of weak character

turbulence : disturbed currents of air, causing vibrations in aircraft

thermal : a rising current of air

traumatised : suffering from severe stress

morbid : unhealthy

simulation : an action or series of actions which are not the real thing e.g. actors might simulate a fight.

8. Discussing Music

Context: 'Tastes in music seem to change from one generation to the next'. This is reflected in the following conversation where Mrs Bhatt, her son Arvind and his friend Shantilal discuss their points of view about different kinds of music.

B : ⎰Isn't it ⎰time we were ⎰booking for the ⎰Charulatha Mani ╱ concert? We ⎰don't want to ⎰leave it ⎰too ⎺late ╱ and ⎰not be able to get ⎺in. Do you re⎰member what ⎰happened when ⎰Ravi Shankar ╱came?

A : ⎰Mother there's a ╲problem. ╱ Would you ⎰mind if I ⎰didn't ╱go?

B : Why ⎰ever ⎺shouldn't you╷ go? ╱ You ⎰don't get a ⎰chance to ⎰hear ⎰people like ⎰Charulatha Mani ⎰every ᵛday. She's been ⎰called almost a ᵛliving ╷symbol ╱ for Car⎰natic ╲Music.

A : ⎰That's partly the ⎺trouble, ╷Ma. ╱ I'm ⎰not really ⎺into Car╷natic ╷Music

S : The ⎰real ᵛdifficulty, Ms ╷Bhatt, ╱ is that there's an ⎰English ⎰group, ⎰Cold ⎺Play ╱ per⎰forming the ⎰same ╷evening. ╱ They're ⎰really ⎺good. ⎰Most of our ⎰friends would ⎰like to ⎰go to ╲that.

B : ⎰What most of your ⎰friends ╱need ╱ is a ⎰musical edu╲cation. ╱ ⎰How you can ⎰listen to that ⎰barbarous ᵛnonsense ╱ is be╲yond me. I'd be ⎰deaf for a ⎺week ╱ if I ⎰went to your ╱concert.

A : It's ⎰not as ⎰bad as all ᵛthat, Ma. It's ⎰not ⎰Hard ⎰Rock or ⎰Heavy ᵛMetal. It's ⎰quite ᵛgentle really. I ⎰think that per⎰haps your di⎰staste for ᵛmodern ╷music ╱ is a gene╲rational thing.

B : Do ╱westerners ⎰listen to our ⎰so-called ╱popular ╷music?

S : ⎺Yes and ╲no.

B : ˈWhat do you mean, ˈyes and ˌno?
S : A ᵛyear ago / I'd have ˈsaid ˌno. The ˈaverage ˈwestern music ˌlover / ˈdidn't ˈlisten to ˈBollywood ˌsound ˌtracks.
B : And ˌnow?
S : ˈSlumdog ˈMillionaire ˈchanged all that. / ˈIndian ˈmusic is ˌin.
B : ˌIn?
S : It's ˈfashionable. There are Punˈjabi and ˈGujarati ˈgroups in ᵛLondon / who ˈdon't neˈglect their own ᵛtraˌditions but inˈcorporate ˈmodern ˈelements as ˌwell. It's ˈcalled ˈfusion ˌmusic.
A : Do you reˈmember the ˌBeatles, Mummy? ᵛOne of them, / ˈGeorge ˌHarrison, / ˈcame to ˈIndia to ˈlearn sitar.
B : And ˈhow ˈlong did he ˈstay?
A : There has ˈusually been ˈcross fertiliˈzation of ˈmusic from ˈdifferent traˌditions. / ˈMother, if we can ˈgo to ˈCold ˌPlay, / I ˈpromise to ˈcome to the ˈnext ˌconcert of Carˌnatic ˌMusic.
B : I'll ˈkeep you to ˈthat.

Glossary

I'm not really into : I don't really like

hard rock, heavy metal : types of popular western music

'in' : fashionable

fusion : joining different elements.

cross fertilization : here features of one kind of music being embedded in another.

9. Student Strikes

Context: One of the beliefs which students in many countries have is that they will change the world, and sometimes indeed they do. Currently, violent demonstrations involving many students in North Africa and the Middle East with most of the violence coming from the authorities, will possibly lead to regime change. Just as often, however, today's firebrand student leader becomes tomorrow's orthodox and respectable politician, and the status quo is preserved.

Mr Menon : I ˈhear the ˈstudents are ˈthreatening to ˈgo on ˏstrike.

Mr Shah : What, aˈ/gain? ˈWhat for ˈthis time?

M : ˈSomething about examiˈnations, I beˏlieve. They ˈwant the ˈpass ˌmark ˌlowered.

S : They'll be ˈasking for deˈgrees to be ˈgiven a ˈway next. They should ˈleave acaˈdemic ˈmatters to the Uniˌversity.

M : It was ˈdifferent in ˈour day ˌ/eh?

S : Well, it ˈwas. We ˈthought we were ˈlucky to be at uniˈversity at ˌall.

M : But we ˈstill went on ˈstrike ocˇcasionally.

S : We had ˈreason to. Our ˈstrikes were ˈpart of the indeˈpendence ˌstruggle.

M : Well, ˈjustified or ˌnot, / we ˈseem to have ˈstarted ˈsomething that has ˈnow beˈcome a ˌhabit.

S : Do you ˈthink our ˈstudents shouldˇnever go on ˌstrike?

M : I supˈpose I ˈwouldn't ˈnecessarily say ˇthat.
  I ˈcan think of ocˌcasions where a ˌstrike might be leˇgitimate, / but it's ˈnot something to be ˈdone indisˈcriminately.

S : You mean the ˈmore this parˈticular ˈweapon is ˌused, / the ˈless efˈfective it beˌcomes?

M : Yes, I ˈdo. ˈThings have now ˈgot into ᵛsuch a state / in ˈsome parts of the ˌcountry / that one's surˈprised to ˌhear / that ocˈcasionally the ˈstudents are ˈnot on strike.
S : You ˈmay be ˈright. ˈCome to ˌthat, / I ˈdon't always ˈthink the auˈthorities ˈhandle the ˈstrikers very ˌwisely. ˈDon't you remˈember that when ˈwe were ˌstudents / ˈnothing ˈirritated us so ˈmuch as ˈranks of poˌlicemen?
M : That's ˈall very ˌwell / but ˈproperty has to be protˈected ˌsomehow.
S : Yes, I ˈknow, / but there ˈmust be ˈmiddle ground ˈsomewhere between reˈpression and ˈanarchy. ˈViolence from ᵛone side / ˈonly breeds ˈmore violence from the ˌ other.
M : That's a ˈgood ˈGandhian ˌstatement.
S : ˈAnyway, / ˈthis isn't a ˈproblem peˈculiar to ˌIndia. ˈLook at ˈwhat's been ˈhappening ˌrecently. There have been ˈstudent demonˈstrations in ˈmany ˌcountries.
M : And in ˈCommunist ˈcountries ˌtoo. ˈLook at ˈChina and the former Czechosloˌvakia.
S : You know I ˈdon't think our ˈchildren ˈvery much ˈlike the ˌway we run the ˌworld for them.
M : ˈNo,/ and ˈsometimes when I ˈlook aˌround /I ˈdon't think I ˈvery much ˌblame them. Well, that's eˈnough ˈmoralising for ˈone ˌmorning. ˈLet's go ˌhome / and ˈget some ˌlunch.
S : ˈOne thing that's ˌcertain / is that our ˈtalking about these ˌproblems / will have ˈno efˈfect whatsoˌever.
M : You know, I think ˈold people like ˌus / have ˈprobably been comˈplaining about the ˈyounger geneᵛration / ˈever since the ˈAryan inˌvasions.
S : ˈEarlier than ˈthat, I ˌshouldn't ˌwonder.

Glossary

firebrand : ardent militant

orthodox : presenting an established viewpoint

status quo : the present position

legitimate : for a good and valid reason

anarchy : when society has broken down

moralising : arguing from a superficially moral viewpoint

10. At the Doctor's

Context: A visit to a doctor's surgery can be a nerve racking business, especially if one does not yet have a diagnosis. Good doctors will communicate with their patients, and try to make them feel comfortable.

Mr Joshi: Good ˇmorning, ˌDoctor.
Dr Chavda: Good ˇmorning, Mr. ˌJoshi. It's quite a ˇwhile / since you've ˈhad to ˈcome and ˌsee me. ˈWhat's the ˇtrouble?
J : I ˈdon't ˇknow ˌreally. ˈEvery ˈnow and aˌgain / I ˈget these atˈtacks of ˌfever.
C : ˇDo you inˌdeed? ˈWhen was the ˇlast one?
J : It's ˈjust ˌfinished. I ˈalmost ˈsent for you two ˇdays ago / but I ˈtreated myself with ˌaspirin / and ˈgot my ˈtemperature ˌdown.
C : And the ˈtime beˈ fore that?
J : ˈThree ˇweeks ago. I've been ˈhaving them ˈevery ˈmonth or so since the ˌwinter.
C : I'd ˈbetter give you a ˈthorough examinˇation then. ˈTake your ˌshirt off / and I'll ˈlisten to your ˌchest.
C : ˈNothing ˈwrong ˇthere. ˈSit ˇdown / and we'll ˈtake your ˌpulse / and ˈsee what your ˇblood pressure's like.
J : ˈQuite a ˈgoing ˇover you're ˌgiving me, / ˇaren't you?
C : Well, we'd ˈbetter ˈget to the ˇbottom of it. We ˈcan't have you going ˇsick every ˌmonth.
* * *
C : ˈBlood -pressure and ˈpulse-rate ˌnormal.
  ˈNurse, / ˈtake Mr.ˈJoshi's ˇtemperature.
N : ˇYes, Doctor. Just ˈpop this under your ˌtongue, / ˌwill you, Mr. ˌJoshi?
* * *

C : Well, what ˈis it?
N : ˈNinety-ˈseven, Doctor.
C : ˈSub-ˈnormal Mr. ˌJoshi; / ˈonly to be exˈpected after ˈall this ˌfever. ˈHow's your ˈappetite been ˌrecently?
J : ˈNot what it ˈmight be, ˌDoctor.
C : What ˈelse have you ˌnoticed when you've been having these atˈtacks?
J : I've had a ˈbit of a ˈsore ˌthroat.
C : Oh, ˈhave you? Well, ˈlet's have a ˌlook at it. ˈPut your head ˌback / and ˈopen your ˌmouth, / ˌwould you? When I ᵛtell you to, / say ˈah'.
C : ˈRight
J : ˈAaaaa . . .
C : Aˈgain.
J : ˈAaaaa . . . ˈAaaaaa . . .
C : Well, it ˈlooks to me as if your ˈtonsils are ˌbadly inˌfected.
J : Do you ˈmean I'll ˈhave to have them ˌout? I'm ˈnot sure I ˈlike ˈthat iˌdea very ˌmuch.
C : It ˈmay be ˈnecessary. But I'll ˈgive you a ˈcourse of anti-biˈotics first/ and we'll ˈsee if ˈthat will ˌclear the inˌfection. Howᵛever, / if you ˈkeep on having ᵛfever, / then you'll ˈhave to have the opeˌration.
J : But ˈthat would mean a ˈlong time off ˈwork, / ˌwouldn't it?
C : Oh, ˌno, /ˈnot very ˌlong. You'd be ˈthree or four ˈdays in my ˌclinic / and then a ˈsimilar ˈperiod at ˌhome. We'd ˈget Dr. ˈRao to do the tonsiˌlectomy. He's ˈvery ˌgood.
J : If it's ᵛgot to be ˌdone / it's ˈgot to be ˈdone, I supˌpose.
C : Now, ˈwhile we're ˌat it, / we'd ˈbetter do aˈblood count.
J : A /what?
C : Aˈblood-count. I'll ˈtake a ˈsample of your ˌblood /and then ˈsend it to the laˈboratory for a ˌnalysis. It ˈtells me

quite a 'lot about your 'general conˬdition. 'Pass me a sy˴ringe, / ˏwill you, ˌnurse.
N : 'Here you ˋare, Doctor.
C : Now 'just 'turn your head a ˋway, / ˏwould you, Mr. Joshi. 'Here we ˋgo.
J : ˋOuch.
C : 'That's ˋthat. 'Now for the peni˴cillin in˯jection / and 'that'll be 'all for toˋday. I'd like you 'back every 'day for the 'next five ˏdays / to com'plete the ˋcourse ˏthough.
J : I'll be 'full of ˋholes, / ˋWon't I?
C : You'll get ˋover it. 'By the ˋway / has your 'youngest 'child been 'vaccinated against diph˯theria?
J : 'No / she ˋhasn't, / though I 'know you've 'done the ˋothers.
C : ˋI ad'vise you to 'bring her ˋin then. There are 'one or two ˋcases aˌbout.

Glossary

nerve racking : making one feel nervous

syringe : a surgical instrument, which should be sterile, used to give vaccinations

blood count : a count of white and red blood cells, among other things, in a patient's blood as an indication of illness or health

A Select Bibliography

1. Bansal, R.K., *The Intelligibility of Indian English*, Monograph No. 4, The English and Foreign Languages University (earlier known as Central Institute of English and Foreign Languages), Hyderabad, second (abridged) edition, 1976, reprinted 1985.
2. Bansal, R.K., 'Teaching Spoken English at Indian Universities', in A.K. Jha and R. Bhargava (eds): *New Directions in English Language Teaching*, Pointer Publishers, Jaipur, 1988.
3. Bansal, R.K., 'The Pronunciation of English in India', in Susan Ramsaran (ed.): *Studies in the Pronunciation of English*, Routledge, London, 1990.
4. Bansal, R.K., 'Teaching of English in the Distance Education System', in Inayat Khan (ed.): *Distance Education: Some Readings*, Amar Prakashan, Delhi, 1991.
5. Bansal, R.K. and Clive Brasnett, *An English Phonetic Reader*/Orient Longman, Calcutta, 1976, second impression, 1989.
6. The English and Foreign Languages University, Hyderabad; *Exercises in Spoken English, Part 1: Accent, Rhythm and Intonation*. Oxford University Press, Madras 1974, Fourth Impression 1985. *Part 2: Consonants*. Oxford University Press, Madras 1977, second impression 1985. *Part 3: Vowels*. Oxford University Press, Madras.
7. *Collins Dictionary of the English Language,* Collins, London, 1979.
8. Gimson, A.C., *An Introduction to the Pronunciation of English*, Edward Arnold, London, 3rd edition, 1980.
9. Jones, Daniel, *English Pronouncing Dictionary*, revised by A.C. Gimson, 14th edition, English Language

Book Society and J.M. Dent & Sons Ltd., London, 1977, reprinted 1981.
10. Sethi, J. and P.V. Dhamija, *A Course in Phonetics and Spoken English* Prentice-Hall of India Private Limited, New Delhi, 1989.